"GIBBY"

"Gibby"

THE RECOLLECTIONS OF A HORSEY MAN

Francis Gibson,
M.B.E.

J. A. Allen
London & New York

ISBN 0-85131-272 2

Published in Great Britain in 1978 by
J. A. Allen & Company Limited,
1, Lower Grosvenor Place, Buckingham Palace Road,
London, SW1W 0EL
and in the United States of America by
Sporting Book Center, Inc.,
Canaan, N.Y.12029.

© Francis Gibson 1978

No part of this book may be reproduced, stored in a retrieval system, or transmitted, in any form or by any means, electronic, mechanical, photocopying, recording or otherwise, without the prior permission of the publishers.

Printed in Great Britain.

FOREWORD

by the Duke of Beaufort, K.G., P.C., G.C.V.O., M.F.H.

It gives me great pleasure to be writing a Foreword to the autobiography of F. E. Gibson, someone well known to me and people attending events like Badminton (he was actually the first stand holder there), horse shows and horse auctions.

Today Gibby has a deserved reputation as a good saddler and over more than half a century he has established himself as a character in the horsey world. He has known many of the giants of that world — beast and man — and has worked with horses as rider, owner and businessman.

Loving horses as he does his memoirs will appeal to anyone who shares that love, and his life has contained adventures of many kinds. Serving in both world wars he saw action from the Somme to the Middle East and in between experienced all the struggles involved in building up his business.

Gibby's life is a story that is thoroughly worth the telling. The pleasure which I have had in reading it makes me recommend it unhesitatingly.

CONTENTS

		Page
FOREWORD by the *Duke of Beaufort*		5
PREFACE		9

Chapter

1	The Quiet American	11
2	The Duchess Disapproves	16
3	The Prince and I	21
4	Song of the Chanteur	25
5	Roll On	33
6	Silent Wedding	37
7	Cock of the North	41
8	American Interlude	44
9	Black Day at Aintree	48
10	The Mysterious Bay	54
11	A Falling Star	58

		Page
12	Desert Command	63
13	Angel on Horseback	69
14	Castles in Spain	73
15	Hat for a Horse	78
16	Princess on the run	81
17	Old pals of mine	84
18	Ride on by	88
	APPENDIX: Saddlery	94
	ACKNOWLEDGEMENTS	122
	INDEX	123

PREFACE

The evenings are the best time of the day for old men such as I. Come the twilight, come the dreams. I have only to close my eyes and I can see the horses and the riders going by . . . that quiet man from America, Danny Maher; the lovable Steve Donoghue; Steve's pal and mine, Tommy Weston who was so much better than he believed; Harry Carr who loves horses more than most; and, of course, the inevitable Lester. All of these, and the hunting and dealing men like Bill Freeman who always looked that much better than anyone on a horse and Tommy Grantham who always seemed to sit a horse differently with his willowy back, in their own ways, have helped colour my days and my nights.

Then from the backrooms of my kind come a motley and ill-assorted band of men . . . Angel Peralta who gained a rare pleasure out of life and yet daily put it at risk; Dobson and Matthew Peacock, those one-time kings of the North; King Edward VII whom I tutored in his wild and princely days; Bertram Mills, that most dapper and punctilious of men; Johnnie Harper and Charlie Reynolds who taught me more about horses than you'll learn from any textbook; and last, but by no means least, Count Ilias Toptani, a dreamer of dreams.

They have, as far as I know, only two things in common. They were part of my life and, like me, they were fascinated by this weird and sometimes wondrous creature known as the horse.

My days have already spanned eight decades and taken me from Wensleydale through the mud of the Somme, the blue grass of Philadelphia, the city of Beirut, a palace in Avila and finally to that horsey kingdom called Newmarket. And in all those places, even in the midst of two World Wars, there were horses at my side. I've never yet known a world without them . . . and I pray I never will.

And if there is one touch of truth, one bit of wisdom I've learnt in all that time, it is this. The horse and the horseman never really change. The horses of my youth are still the horses I meet today, motivated by the same fears and the same pleasures. If you understood them then, you understand them now. The men upon their backs may possibly have become a little kinder, a little more enlightened. But the fascination remains unchanged.

I listened to Lester Piggott recently at the end of a long, hard season. He was wearing that grey, harrowed look he so often wears with the coming of autumn. Someone asked him why he continued to ride on when there were, after all, no fresh worlds to conquer. He considered the question for a moment, then he shrugged and said, "What else would I do with my days? Where else could I find that kind of pleasure?"

To me, the words had a familiar ring and then I remembered. I had heard them half a century earlier from the lips of Danny Maher . . . and that is where this book begins.

CHAPTER ONE

THE QUIET AMERICAN

*God forbid that I should go to any
heaven in which there were no horses.*

R. B. CUNNINGHAM-GRAHAM

It was one of those September days when the world has a tranquil face. From my bed in the nursing home, I could look out across the roofs of London to Regents Park. The leaves were falling and I could see children playing. But for me, at least, this peaceful scene would be shortlived. It was 1915 and Europe was at war. The trenches had been dug on the Somme and the big guns were scarring the land. As soon as I had recovered from my operation, I too would be heading for the front. There was a rumour that the war would be over by Christmas and I wondered whether this could be true. I was still wondering when the door opened and Danny Maher walked in.

Noel Leach, of Newmarket, a relation of Felix Leach, was on one side of him and Maher's wife, the musical comedy star Doreen Frazer, on the other. They had their arms around him and clearly he needed the support. He was pale as a ghost and his legs seemed to bow with every step. The climb up the stairs to my top-floor room had been sufficient to bring about this near collapse.

I asked him whether he would like me to ring for a brandy. He half-smiled and shook his head.

"No, it's a kind thought," he said. "But don't worry

about me. I just had a bit of a wild night, that's all." He didn't fool any of us. Even at the age of nineteen, I could recognise a deathly sick man when I saw one. I told him that I had seen his winning ride on Bayardo in the St. Leger and this seemed to act as a tonic of a kind.

The colour was beginning to return and he said, "Yes, that was an easy horse to ride, the kind who'll stay for ever. We could have gone another couple of furlongs. No trouble at all." This was the way he always talked about his races. Like so many of life's champions, he made it all sound and look too easy. He rode most of his big winners out with hands and heels and you hear the punters say, "Well, anyone could have won on that horse. The Yank just went along for the ride."

He is often linked in people's minds with his fellow American, Tod Sloan. But the two men had little in common. They were as different as the night is to the day. Sloan was flamboyant and brash both on and off a horse. He was one of the first monkey-up-a-stick jockeys to come to Europe. He smoked big, black, evil-looking cigars, even in the parade ring. And his style of dress made the average bookmaker look very conservative indeed.

Maher, by contrast, was a quiet man and a quiet rider with the most beautiful hands and no great lover of the whip. He rode with his leathers at what the jockeys of the day considered a sensible length and he was twice the horseman that Sloan could ever hope to be.

His style of dress was as modest as the man. He favoured dark suits and dark waistcoats, cut in the English style. And although diamond stickpins and gold watchchains were looked upon as racing's badge of success at the time, I never saw him wear either.

In view of these quiet ways, it seemed surprising that he won himself such a bride. For Doreen Frazer had been very literally the toast of the town during her days at the Lyceum. She was a long-legged hoyden of a girl, very striking with long, black, silken hair and the hour-glass type of figure that all women aspired to. The more I saw her, the more I liked her. And under a rather brash front, there was a kind heart and there could be no doubting her concern for poor Danny.

He visited me several times in the weeks that followed and we naturally talked about racing. On one occasion, I asked him whether he thought Sloan's syle would ever catch on and his answer surprised me.

He said, "Yes, one day I think it will. But you need to have good balance to ride that way. I tried it for a while back in the States and found that I couldn't keep my horses running straight. I needed my legs for that. But Sloan is not considered unusual back home. We have a lot of jockeys who ride even shorter. There's a fellow called Sims who practically stands on the back of his horses."

Danny had been champion jockey in the last year before the war and since then had limited his racing. But he still rode and you didn't need to be a medical man to know that he should instead have been sitting in a deckchair in some quiet garden with a rug wrapped around him.

On what was to be our last day together, I asked him why he did insist on riding against the advice of his doctors. I said, "After all, Danny, you've won everything that matters and estsablished a reputation that the years can never dim. Why not rest up for a while and then come back after the war, stronger and better than ever?"

He reached out and patted me on the shoulder. "You're a well-meaning young man," he said. "But you don't really understand. Horses are my life. A world in which I couldn't get up on to the back of a horse would be no world at all. Racing gives me the only true pleasure I know . . ."

And then remembering that his wife was by his side, he smiled and added, "Apart, of course, from my days with Doreen."

It was, in fact, a day of mutual concern. Maher had just learnt from Noel Leach that I was to sail for France at the weekend. "But damn it all, Gibby," he said. "You've barely had time to convalesce. At least, get well before you go to that hellish place."

I was touched that, at such a moment in his life, he could be concerned about someone else. For by then, we both knew he had consumption and was a dying man.

And I'll admit that I too didn't look upon France with any enthusiasm, mainly because I knew too little about the actual mechanics of the guns I would probably be expected to fire. This was due to the lectures on gunnery being too often interrupted by the Riding Master, Lieutenant Hance a former rough riding Bombardier, sending for me to go to the riding school to give a display. I had seen the casualty lists from the Somme. I had also seen the wounded coming home on the troopships . . . some seemingly almost glad to have lost an arm in return for an escape from the battle.

On arrival in France, I was posted as a Second-Lieutenant to the Guards Divisional Artillery — a division that was moved around a great deal — and then joined a divisional ammunition column. Almost every evening, we would go up the line from our camp near Poperinghe to the Ypres Salient, delivering ammunition with six-horse waggons.

It was a messy job and resulted in the loss of men and horses . . . getting bogged down and temporarily lost. We would frequently return to camp, very bedraggled, snatch a few hours sleep after dealing with the horses, and then have to set off again for Ypres. It was about this time that the Prince of Wales visited our lines with Louis Grieg, his equerry, and we had quite a chat. I was later moved to Major Alan Cunningham's battery. In the Second World War, he achieved some fame as a major-general and was also knighted.

This was my first experience of front-line warfare, living in dug-outs and manning observation posts, the wires of which were eternally being cut by enemy gunfire.

Some people have an almost total recall of the war days. I only remember the misery, the futile running across open ground, the price paid to gain a few yards of useless land and then, in no time at all, the getting back again. I don't think many of us expected to come out of that alive. It wasn't a question of will I die? Only of when?

Finally we moved up to Passchendaele, having taken over another battery's guns. This posed problems, as we didn't know their peculiarities and so were always terrified by the idea of dropping shells "short" on our own infantry. By then, we had lost so many officers that I found myself commanding a six-gun battery. I was still only nineteen. But it's surprising how rapidly you come of age in a situation like that.

I became all too accustomed to death. They were often friends with whom I'd been sharing a joke just a few hours earlier. One such was young de Courcy Parry, the brother of "Dalesman", who loved horses almost as much as I.

Then one day, there came a letter from home with the news that Danny Maher was dead. You might well imagine that with so much death around me, it would have meant very little. But it moved me greatly. I had grown very fond of this quiet American.

He was such a rare talent that it wasn't, in my opinion, until the coming of Lester Piggot, that we had a jockey capable of replacing him.

I wrote a stumbling letter of condolences to his widow. Battery commander or not, I was still too young to know what to say.

CHAPTER TWO

THE DUCHESS DISAPPROVES

*Whene'er I come and whene'er I go
I get a smile from Rosa.
Perhaps a kiss or two or so,
At three she answers "No sir!"*

ANON

I walked into the Cavendish Hotel towards the close of a rain-filled day in the spring of 1916 . . . and almost walked straight out again. Surveying the scene over the rim of a champagne glass was the hotel's owner, Rosa Lewis.

Fortunately I elected to stay. Otherwise I would have missed a slice of life and a memory that I treasure. If the Cavendish was remarkable, so too was Rosa, popularly known in those days as "The Duchess of Jermyn Street." Rumour had it that she had been the mistress of both King Edward VII and the Kaiser. True to her nature, she neither confirmed nor denied such stories. Her love affairs were always very discreet and one of her favourite sayings was, "No letters, no lawyers and kiss my baby's bottom." But certainly they had both been friends of hers. She had her corsets autographed by Edward to prove it and was a guest of the Kaiser on his private yacht, *The Hohenzollern*.

With the coming of war, she had turned the hotel into what was virtually a home from home for the troops. The Irish Guards were her particular favourites, but she had a warm spot in that big heart of hers for any fighting man. Just about any, that is, except me.

She seemed to disapprove of me from the very beginning. And several times I turned unexpectedly to find her glaring balefully in my direction. I hadn't too much time to puzzle this out. There were other more pressing matters on my mind. I had been sent home on compassionate leave, because my father was very ill. He was being treated at Mundesley in Norfolk for something not too terribly serious and dying from something not diagnosed. Still at the time, it all seemed like a false alarm and so, after visiting him, I was free to enjoy my brief stay at the Cavendish before returning to France.

The place had begun to fascinate and so too, from a distance did Rosa. Her soft brown hair was already edged with grey, but she was still a beautiful and commanding woman. A latter-day Nell Gwynn.

Although she had friends in high places, she made little or no attempt to disguise her Cockney origin. She still spoke in the clipped accents of her youth, with an enunciation all her own. She had this odd habit of placing an "r" between a consonant and a vowel. Thus balcony became "bralcony" and Gibby eventually turned into "Gribby". I once heard her describe her ex-husband as "a bit of a dud," while bounced cheques were always "stumers" to her. She also had a habit of muddling people's names. Caroll Carstairs, for instance, was addressed alternately as "Mr. Cardboard" and "Mr. Carsteps," although his correct name always appeared on the bill.

Rosa was a big woman and, when she wished, a formidable one. Like many ladies of the time, she had developed the quirk of sending white feathers to men who hadn't gone to the front. The Kaiser had once given her a large, signed portrait of which she had once been very proud. Now it had been relegated to the gentlemen's cloakroom with the words, "That's the only throne for old Willy."

Although Rosa never rode, she had a definite affection for horsemen. The remarkable Sir Claude Champion de Crespigny was a particular favourite. It would be difficult to find a more foolhardy fellow. He was involved in brawls with sundry waiters and taxi-drivers around town. He was the first to cross the North Sea in a balloon, having broken both legs on a previous attempt. When he swam the Nile rapids, he dived in amongst the crocodiles. His career as an amateur steeplechase jockey followed a similarly wild pattern. In 1880, mounted on Brown Tommy in the Essex Hunt Cup at Colchester, he fell twice but won the race. Although said to be "a mad rider", he did at least take the precaution of walking the course before every race-day. He often competed with Bay Middleton, but said in his memoirs that this famous horseman had one bad fault . . . "He spurred his horse in the shoulder, being apparently unable to sit a horse without turning his toes out."

Some rather more conventional riders who became an established part of the Rosa Lewis circle were the members of the American polo team which took Europe by storm in the early part of the twentieth century. She made sure that they always stayed at the Cavendish when visiting England.

Rosa adored these clean-cut, rich and lively young men . . . Devereux Milburn, Watson Webb, Charles Rumsey, Len Stoddard and Tommy Hitchcock, of whom she was particularly fond. When they were in residence, the Cavendish took on the atmosphere of a hilarious houseparty.

But if the hotel bore a strange and eccentric air at times, you can be sure it was because Rosa wished it that way. She had a liking for characters and it showed.

She had a hall porter called Steffany who would have found it hard to land a job in any other hotel in the land, but at the Cavendish he was a star attraction. He wore a greasy tail-coat, a tea-stained dicky, was deaf and nearly blind. He was described variously as the former bodyguard to the Emperor Maximilian, a butler to the Rothschilds, a soldier with Garibaldi and Rosa's first lover. No one knows how these rumours originated, for he spoke to no-one.

Another hall porter was known as "Dirty Scott", because of his rooted objection to having a bath. Rosa was always giving him notice. But when he was in her bad books, Lord Ribblesdale always defended him and he stayed at the Cavendish for years.

The oddest things always seemed to be happening at the Cavendish. On one occasion, a young writer was having a bath when the door burst open and Rosa marched in with two visitors. The writer, a modest young man, stared at the couple in stark disbelief and they regarded him with similar emotions. But Rosa, no way phased by all this, continued her guided tour talk by saying, "Five guineas a day, the young chap not included."

One day when I went down to the office to pay my bill, I found Rosa there, the inevitable yellow beads around her neck, the equally inevitable champagne glass in her hand. She was having an argument with another guest, which she climaxed by saying, "You treat my house like a hotel," which to say the least was scarcely encouraging.

Then she turned to me, with blood in her eye as the saying goes, and snapped, "Well, what do you want?" I told her I'd come to pay the bill and she shrugged shoulders which had been described as the most beautiful in London.

"It's not ready," she said, still in the mood for a fight. "We'll have to send it on to you."

I said, "I'm afraid you can't do that. You see I'm off this morning and I may not be back for a while."

"Off? Off where?"

"To France. I have to rejoin my unit tonight."

The transformation in Rosa was both instant and remarkable. Her face softened and she placed a hand on my shoulder.

"My dear boy," she said. "Why didn't you tell me. I thought you were one of those bloody draft dodgers. If only I'd known, we could have been such pals."

And then with the changeable mood so typical of her, she said, "You really should have told me. You make me feel so bad about it. After all, how could I be expected to know. You arrive here in mufti and I never once heard you mention the war." She somehow made all this sound like an accusation.

I explained that I'd wanted to forget about the fighting for a while . . . that talking about it gave me no pleasure at all. And at this, she nodded.

"Yes," she said. "I can understand that. Where's your unit?"

I told her that it was at Passchendaele and at this I had the impression that she was very close to tears.

"My God, you're so young. If only I'd known, I'd have brought you a champagne breakfast in bed. That's what I do, you know, when my young men go back to France."

I was still in some awe of her and anxious to be gone. So I said that I had to be at Victoria Station in half-an-hour and suggested that she guessed at what the bill should be.

She turned on me quite fiercely and said, "You're not paying any money in my hotel. I'll get it off these so-and-so's who are hanging around here at home."

Then softening once more, she said, "Come on. Let's find you a taxi. And you must promise to come and stay here next time you're on leave. We'll have a drink and a lot of laughs together. I'll make you happy. You'll see I will."

She walked me out into Jermyn Street with her arm tucked into mine, flapped an arm and a taxi arrived instantly. She then kissed me on both cheeks, reminded me of my promise to come and see her again and waved me goodbye.

At the end of Jermyn Street, I looked back. She was still standing there, yellow beads glinting in the sunlight . . . and still waving.

CHAPTER THREE

THE PRINCE AND I

*Fain would I ride but that I fear to fall
If you're afraid, then do not ride at all.*

SIDNEY

There were soft lights and the melody of a foxtrot, as the music played in our chateau, high on an Italian hillside. All I needed to make the evening perfect was a beautiful girl floating in my arms. Instead my partner was Edward, Prince of Wales and he was in a prickly mood.

"Damn it, Gibby," he said. "You've got it wrong again. How can I hope to improve, if you keep on missing the step?"

I could have pointed out that I normally lead when I danced and that I just wasn't used to doing it the other way around. But I said nothing. It seemed wisest that way. And I guessed that he was probably feeling as foolish as the rest of us. A dance without women just wasn't a dance at all. Still apart from this, there was little to complain about. Corps Headquarters in Italy was a far cry from the mud of Passchendaele and I counted myself a very lucky man to have made the switch.

It had all come very literally out of a clear blue sky. One moment, I'd been sweltering under the sun with my battery at the front. The next, I'd been whisked down to St. Omer by General Wardrop. He put me in charge of a force which had to deliver a large amount of ammunition to our army in Italy, which was under the command of Lord Cavan.

He told me, "I'm putting a big responsibility on your

shoulders. That ammunition is needed desperately. So speed is absolutely essential. I know you won't let me down."

We had a hundred lorries, all three-tonners, absolutely packed with ammunition of all kinds. We picked the most direct route possible and drove down through parts of France, where they hadn't seen any British troops before. We were given the most tumultuous welcome all along the route. The offers of hospitality were sumptuous. Bottles of wine were pushed into our hands. And girls were waving and calling out to the troops, possibly with offers of a different kind. I didn't make myself very popular by insisting that we kept continually on the move . . . restricting the hours of sleep to the barest minimum.

As it was we arrived very much in the manner of the U.S. Cavalry. Just in time with the batteries running desperately low with their ammunition. I was later decorated for this with the Crown of Italy, which my wife wears on a chain today. I was also promoted to staff captain. One of my duties was to arrange for the ammo to be taken up the mountains (near the Piave river) on Teleferica (overhead) railways and also by pack mules.

I used to go riding with the Prince of Wales and he was quite ready to listen to advice. He was lacking in all the natural talents of a horseman. He was keen, tremendously so, and he was brave. But those two qualities operated against him. He was in too much of a hurry to learn and almost euphoric at times.

His thighs were large and this doesn't help. It was impossible to instill caution. I used to select a reasonably docile animal for him, one I trusted completely. All he had to do was just go along for the ride and let the horse make all the decisions. But he was forever trying to take fences too fast . . . and forever paying the price. And when he did fall, he tended to hit the ground very hard indeed. He had more than one bad fall but, lacking the athlete's natural grace, seemed unable to master the art of rounding the shoulder and rolling. If he was too brave on a horse, the Prince was also too brave in his day-to-day affairs. It was almost as though he was determined to court disaster. He had a habit, for instance, of wandering too near the Austrian lines as he drove around the various front-line positions, at a time when we knew they had patrols probing deep into Italian territory. On one occasion, at least, he persuaded the Canadian pilot, Barker, to fly him over the lines. It was a day of bright sunlight and the sort when the Austrian airmen were in the habit of flying up into the sun's direct rays and then swooping down with the protecting light behind them.

The Prince and I were of a similar age and, although I liked him — it was impossible not to — I never really understood him. We used to talk at great length, but he never seemed to say anything which you remembered at the end of the day.

I don't think he was ever very good at communicating with his fellow men. I suspect that it was only with women that he revealed his secret heart.

One of the ironies of his service in Italy was that just about every match-making matron in the land was anxious for the Prince to meet her daughter . . . and he was only too willing to oblige. But that most serious of men, Lord Cavan, supreme commander of the Anglo-Italian forces, was equally determined to ensure that he stayed with us at Army H.Q. He and his Chief of Staff, were always careful to keep an eye on the Prince.

Lord Cavan was a small, tubby, mild man and not easy to talk to — as I found whenever he took me as his aide-de-camp to Milan races. His own aide-de-camp was non-horsey, so I was considered more suitable.

On one occasion I arranged dinner at a restaurant and told the management that the Commando Supremo was arriving at 8 p.m. and to ensure they put on a good show. Flowers, carpet, and so on.

Cavan inspired considerable respect at headquarters, but he could be very human, as I was to discover on this occasion.

Perhaps the effort made by the restaurant had had the desired effect, for Cavan unbent a little. He had been a keen amateur rider and told me that he had become an excellent judge of pace. "Do you know how I did it, Gibson?" he said.

I shook my head in an encouraging sort of way.

"Well, I used to walk along the street and then I'd see some fellow coming towards me from some distance off. I'd pick a lamp-post between us and change my pace, so that we'd both arrive there at the same time."

He paused, fixing me with a stern eye. "Mind you. You've got to be straight with yourself. No cheating. No sudden scurrying at the last moment. Otherwise you'll never learn."

Oddly enough, the Australian jockey, Rae Johnstone, also improved his judgment of pace in this way. And Johnstone, remember, was one of the finest timers of a finish in racing history. Hence the nickname bestowed on him in France of "Le Crocodile." He used to gobble them up on the post.

I must admit it wasn't a bad war for us just then and a great change from France. Among the horse units I remember people like Bill Payne (senior), Dick Young (Carlisle), Jim Mitchell (Penrith) and Billy Saxby (jockey).

I was also in the same mess as Lord Castlerosse who proved a great raconteur, Gaythorne Hardy and Lord Derby's son, Lord Stanley. There were races and show-jumping events and gradually the war was coming to an end . . . and it should be remembered what a very important part this Italian front played in the outset. For when the Allies eventually broke through, over the Piave and into Austria, it proved to be the turning point of the entire war.

After the Armistice, General Wardrop very kindly offered to get me a regular commission. And I, very foolishly, turned this down. Instead I headed for home, saying goodbye to many friends and two chargers of whom I had become very fond.

CHAPTER FOUR

SONG OF THE CHANTEUR

My business is my pleasure
My pleasure is my business

ANON

It was a cheerless homecoming. My Quaker-bred parents had both died by now, while I was sadly faraway. My friends had scattered. I was jobless and soon to be homeless too. For the old colonel from whom we'd rented our house in Wensleydale now wished to return.

Like many men back from the war, I felt terribly unsettled. My grandparents would have liked me to join Barclays Bank, which had taken over our family bank (Gibson, Tuke and Gibson). But my father had left me with a bit of advice which, if followed, can prove more precious than jewels. "Let your pleasure be your business," he was fond of saying. "And your business your pleasure."

To me, this could only be interpreted in one way. I would work with horses and, in that day and age, that really meant becoming a dealer.

At least, I had had a good grounding. Although born in Cambridge four years before the turn of the century, we had moved north when I was only two. We used to spend our winters in Darlington, where my father was Chief at the bank, and our summers in Wensleydale. I was riding my first pony across Pen Hill at an early age.

Whenever I was home from Malvern School, I seemed to be

mingling with the horsey crowd. I used to have tea at Brecongill with that Grand Old Man of racing, Johnnie Osborne. And was allowed to ride out with Nat Scott's string of racehorses at Tupgill, later the home of Robert Armstrong, father of Gerald and Sam. I well remember my first meet at Denton Crossroads, just north of Darlington, with Will Freeman hunting the Zetland Hounds. No man ever looked better in the saddle than Will.

But my true education came through working with the great horse dealers of the day, men such as Johnnie Harper and Charlie Reynolds. I learnt things with them that I could have learnt nowhere else.

Johnnie had a first-class small hunter business at Dalton Terrace, York, and a very loyal following. His horses were not expensive and he catered for people wanting hunters with manners. A very personal business and he was greatly respected. I began my career as a dealer by going to work for him directly after the First World War.

I remember well we were not supposed to whistle as this was considered cheeky, but singing was quite all right and was presumably regarded as proof of our contentment.

There was an odd-shaped yard with about twenty-five boxes, and these had drains in their centres, all plugged. A large quantity of sawdust was in each box with straw on top. Sawdust is excellent bedding when there is plenty of labour to pick up the wet patches, and saves much straw. Incidentally, it is also handy for making animals appear slightly larger or smaller at will, as I was to find out later in another dealer's yard.

"Bringing a horse to the door," which was a term for showing a customer a horse, was quite an act which had to be learnt thoroughly, and each horse was shown in a short cheek double bridle (ready for the ride, if the customer so wished). The horse was then led to a platform of broken brick with a buff-coloured frame at the back. One was expected to get him on his legs at the first attempt, with no pushing back or pulling forward.

You kept your eyes more or less on the horse with an occasional look at Johnnie. And in a moment or two a stableman at the end of the yard would be raising a stable rubber or a fork to make him cock his ears. You then walked off without any jogging to show how well he walked down a cinder path with a pergola of roses either side. Then he was jogged back very quietly and finally you were before your customer again, where you waited for the words "We will just see a saddle on him" . . . and you were off to the box for the man to pop the saddle on.

The men would hiss a good deal — they always did so when grooming, to keep dust from the horse's coat and it was such a habit that a groom would not think he was doing his job unless he was hissing — wipe your horse over and rub your boots, and you were then again ready to give your little ridden show. The whole idea was to prove that the horse had excellent manners, as he probably had. Johnnie was a real and true lover of horses and everything was managed with unhurried skill. You walked, trotted and cantered round the cinder track. And by the second time around, one of the men had wheeled out a little fence, which you negotiated with as loose a rein as possible. This performance went on sometimes almost hourly during busy times such as York Race week, and I have pulled the same horse to the door many times in a single day.

I say everything was peaceful, well it usually was, but I remember a very unpleasant business which nearly ended my stay with Johnnie. I had been asked to show some hunters to Frank Wilkinson of Edwinstowe, a very astute dealer. He was catching an early train and I was naturally in a hurry to please him. I had ridden one horse and put him back in the stable rather quickly, as another horse was saddled and ready for me.

But after having ridden the second one twice round the cinder track, I was alarmed to see something I took to be smoke coming through the ventilator of the previous horse's box. I quickly made some excuse and, upon reaching the box, saw to my horror that the horse was going round like a ball. He had kicked at a fly on his belly and caught his toe in a stirrup iron.

It was a very terrifying business and the last time that I ever left a horse with stirrup irons down. Sawdust, cement and sparks were flying in all directions. Happily the bar of the saddle came away and he was free, standing there somewhat dazed with a few cuts and bumps on him.

Frank Wilkinson came up and, pressing a coin into the palm of my hand, advised me to get out of the yard as quickly as possible . . . and to stay away, until I was sent for. I went back to my bed-sitting room and waited, feeling very miserable, until about midday when one of the strappers called and told me I was to come back after my meal, as the "missus" had pleaded for me. For some days afterwards, I was reminded of my foolish blunder by seeing odd painters and decorators putting the box in order. And I was bandaging and using kaolin on the horse's swellings for some days.

Johnnie, incidentally, had a unique and very effective method of placing bandages around the joints of horses. He never bandaged up to the knee and always used a square of gauze tissue with bound edges which lasted a long time.

Whenever he went into the box, he would brush up the back of the horses' legs with a dandy brush to increase the look of the "bone". He never clipped the top of a horse's withers, and would carefully decide whether a mane was to be left or not.

Few, if any, horses get sore withers from their rugs if people refrain from clipping on top of withers. Johnnie Harper's rugs also had two sections of thick felt on either side of the rug at the withers to take the weight. Many years later, during the Second World War in fact, I was to be reminded of Johnnie's excellent example. During my service in the Middle East, I was responsible for a very large number of Transport horses who were equipped with breast harness. We had quite a spate of sore withers at one time and, having discussed the matter with "Mouse" Townsend — our head vet — we left all horses unclipped on top of the withers, and were free from this trouble ever after.

Johnnie Harper also had an unusual, but again highly

effective, method of curing nappy horses. After an animal had behaved in a disobedient manner, one dismounted, slipped off the saddle, fixed the roller and hobbles . . . and then "threw" the horse quietly (preferably on to grass or peat), tied up his legs and walked away. No stick, just a very definite snub and it was surprising how well it worked.

I remember showing a grey horse to a customer who had not "napped it" for six months and was seemingly cured. When the prospective customer, who had been told of the horse's previous indiscretions, put his hand on his foreleg, he started to go down . . . so used had he become to being put on the floor. The customer just said, "He seems to want to say his prayers." In America, this is known as the Beery method. Every day seemed to extend my education. There was so much to learn for those with eyes to see.

One day in 1931, I visited Aldridges Horse Repository (purchased from Beesons in 1770) in St. Martins Lane, London with my uncle, Alexander Gibson, who was a hunting man. He spotted a hunter from the Puckeridge Hunt country in the sale. The hunter had built up a reputation as a runaway but was sold for around £25 to a hansom cab driver, naturally without a warranty. My uncle took the driver to a pub nearby and warned him about the horse. The driver, a remarkably cheery chap, chuckled. "That's all right, Guv," he said. "I'll be able to handle him. No trouble at all."

My uncle, something of a gambling man, studied the cabbie thoughtfully.

"I wouldn't put any money on that, if I was you," he advised.

The cabbie, clearly a gambling man too, took a sip of his beer and said, "Tell you what, guv. You look like a sport to me. So tell me where you'll be tomorrow night and I'll pick you up with this 'ere horse and deliver you safe and sound to wherever you want to go. A fiver says I can do it."

"I'll be at the Eccentric Club in Ryder Street," said Uncle Gibson.

The following evening, the cabbie duly arrived with the

horse that was as good as gold . . . and my astonished uncle paid up. The cabbie took us on, I remember, to the old Holborn Empire where we saw G. H. Elliott — the "Chocolate Coloured Coon". The horse behaved impeccably on the journey and we then learnt the cabbie's secret. He had fitted his horse with a nose net. In later years, I found that this was a useful device to sell to owners of difficult animals, when all else had failed.

Quite recently, a trainer in the north telephoned and asked my advice on how best to get a jockey safely down to the starting gate on a real tearaway of a horse. I suggested a net — adding that he should then ask permission from the stewards for the starter's assistant to remove this on arrival.

I wish I could end this story by saying that the horse won the race, but I cannot. He was second!

Virtually every dealer I have known had at least one method he relied upon. Willie Lancaster of Brompton, near Northallerton, for instance, believed in "grunting" any prospective purchase. This was a rough and ready way of testing for wind, and known as "threatening" years ago. He would pretend to hit the horse and assume that if he or she grunted or sighed, the animal was unsound. Willie was seldom proved wrong.

Oliver Dixon, whom I knew well, had a big yard with a lot of Irish horses at Reading and catered for Army officers a great deal. He taught me several little tricks and one impressed me particularly. He would be standing under the rostrum in Tattersalls when perhaps polo ponies were being sold. He would then go up to the pony, put his forefinger in its mouth and purely by touch would be able to tell if the bars of the mouth were hardened, if the tongue was too big for the tongue groove and also what age the pony was. Just in that one movement.

Another odd pearl of wisdom came from Harry Beeby, who excelled as both dealer and horseman. He once told me that he didn't care for these "Swanny" necked animals. He said, "I prefer horses with good shoulders and with shorter necks which are more easily steered in the right direction."

During those embryo dealing days of mine, I became equally interested in the activities of the "Chanteur", although I realised that their method of doing business was highly undesirable. These men were certainly villains, but their activities may amuse my readers. The name was used because they could sing a good song!

The Chanteur (often miscalled Chanter), with larceny in mind, had first to buy a suitable animal. Let's say he was going to sell what in those days were "ride and drive" horses or cobs. He would need to find one that was good looking and appeared sound, but had in fact a very big defect . . . what is known as a horse with a big hole in him. Perhaps the trouble would be kicking, nappiness (gibbing), going lame when in real work or maybe again a horse that was "over the bridge" (having a defective back) or a shiverer . . . the latter could sometimes become evident after a rail journey.

Well, the chanteur would take a small stable on a very short lease in a residential part of town and proceed to advertise a "lovely, dapple-grey horse, quiet to ride and drive," and so on. The customers would call by appointment and our chanteur . . . perhaps acting now the part of a solicitor's clerk and instructed to sell his deceased client's valuable animal . . . would make the deal and take the money, in cash naturally.

Then a colleague would discover the home of the purchaser and, if necessary, take up lodgings nearby. So that he would be on hand to witness the distressing scene of the horse's nappiness, over-turned gig, shafts broken, and the like. He would then offer to help the unfortunate purchaser . . . saying that it just so happened that he had a nephew who bought such misfits. And so the animal would be repurchased at a ridiculously low figure, and sometimes the purchaser would even pay his "benefactor" for taking the horse off his hands.

After regaining their animal, the chanteur and his accomplice would move their operation to another town . . . and the disgraceful business would begin all over again.

But of course the majority of advertisers, then and now,

were totally honest. And none more so than Charlie Reynolds, a dealer with yards all over London and one of the great characters of the early 1900s. He had started in a humble way, being a shoeing smith, and was clever at improving the action of horses.

By the time I came to know him, he had established a very fine business and supported all the Fortnum and Mason transport. Later he turned to Model T Fords and bought many chassis and fitted box bodies to suit commercial travellers in the rag trade.

I don't think I ever knew a more honest man, or a kinder one. He seemed, at times, quite incapable of telling a lie and he treated me like a favoured son. I owe Charlie a very great deal.

I have one of his advertisements beside me now, extracted from an old *Field* periodical:

"STELLA, a remarkably-handsome Dark Brown high-stepping, Norfolk-bred Mare, 6 years 15.2 hands, has plenty of bone and quality: quiet to ride and drive in single and double harness, free and fast and grand all-round mover, winner of three prizes in harness for pace and action, a pleasure to drive, up to 16st. in saddle, and carries a lady; thoroughly accustomed to motor cars &c., and warranted sound; been driven in Victoria and Ralli car in town and country; price 45 gns; one month's trial allowed. Apply to Mr. C. Reynolds, 2A, Hamfrith Road, off Romford Road, Stratford, Essex."

If Charlie said all that, you can be quite sure of one thing. Stella was a beauty.

CHAPTER FIVE

ROLL ON

Roll on. Thou Ball. Roll on
Through seas of inky air. Roll on
It's true I have no shirts to wear
It's time my butcher's bill is due
It's true my prospects all look blue
But don't let that unsettle you
Never you mind. Roll on!

ANON

Cliff Walton was one of those fellows who are eternally reaching for the moon. He was a buyer for Giles (Ben) Bishop and he wanted the best of everything . . . and for Giles only the best would do.

At that time Giles was the most fashionable hunter dealer in the south of England, and Cliff surrounded himself with the best horses, the best cars and naturally the best women. He was a handsome man with oceans of style and the ladies adored him.

He had just such a girl with him when I met him one day at a horse sale in Norwich. In no time at all, you would have imagined that they were lifelong friends. She was very refined and, as we returned to the station, to catch the London train, I felt as though I was walking on egg-shells. I didn't know what sort of story Cliff had spun her and, if this was his dream, I had no wish to dent it.

The three of us went through the barrier and, at that moment, who should spot us but, of all people, Ted Martindale, a dealer from Hillmorton, near Rugby. I say "of all people", because Ted, although a great pal of ours, was scarcely the most tactful of men . . . as he proceeded to prove.

He promptly shouted out, "Hurry up, Cliff, we'll find an empty carriage. And bring the tart with you."

"Did he say 'tart'?" enquired our lady, sounding more refined than ever.

Cliff shrugged, more in sorrow than in anger.

"Poor old chap," he said. "You mustn't take any notice of him."

In fact, it was the sort of situation, which appealed to Cliff's sense of humour immensely . . . and, in fact, inspired another incident.

A few days later when Cliff and I were in Leicester, we discovered that Joe Trowers (Charlie Reynolds' partner) had a villa in Brighton and would sometimes let a couple of rooms to fellow dealers. Now Joe was a very straight-laced man who disapproved strongly of Cliff's high-wheeling ways. Still, on this occasion, Cliff greeted him in a very respectful fashion. And after a bit of horsey conversation, mentioned that he and I would be down in Brighton at the weekend and asked whether we could maybe rent a couple of rooms. Joe said it was OK with him and looked forward to seeing us.

Cliff thanked him, still very respectful and then mentioned very casually that we would need double beds as we were bringing two girls down with us. Joe, outraged, began to splutter and Cliff, pretending to misunderstand, patted him on the shoulder. And with that, he turned and walked away. Joe was so angry that he just couldn't get the words out for a moment or two. And then he shouted at Cliff's departing back, "You come anywhere near that house of mine and I'll shoot you. I mean it. I really will."

I think he would have too.

But that was the irreverent humour that was so very typical of the world of the horse dealer. They were frequently a rough and ready lot with their own rather fanciful brand of ethics.

Yet they were also larger-than-life characters who live on in the mind.

I remember, for instance, a well-known and reputable Belfast hunter dealer with a very lively sense of fun. And one day at Leicester Sales, he became interested in the horse of a very fierce-looking old farmer. The farmer insisted that the horse was perfect.

"Perfect?" repeated our Irish friend, raising his eyebrows in mock astonishment. "In all my days, I've never met a perfect horse."

"Well, you have now," said the farmer, growing very red of face. And to prove the point, he handed over the reins. The Irishman began to canter around the cinder track and almost immediately, loud and clear, came a most distinct "whistling".

The farmer's expression was one of blank astonishment. He shook his head, as though hoping he'd wake up and find that this had all been part of some terrible dream.

Dick Young who, at one time, had been the most successful dealer in the North was standing beside me. And this was all too much for him. He started to laugh and said to the Irishman, "You can't do this to the old boy."

And then, of course, the truth came out. The dealer had been the culprit . . . and ventriloquising. He began to laugh too. "No, you're right," he said. "I can't. But it did help to brighten the day a little, didn't it?"

Harold Field of Chichester was a quite brilliant judge of a horse. And I remember his foreman-cum very good nagsman, George Sadler, telling me once that his boss was a better judge of a horse, with a rug on and a hundred yards away, than most dealing men were of one, rugless and close up. I believe that too.

But Harold had a sardonic humour that could be almost cruel at times, as the following story suggests.

Once when visiting a Welsh farm, he stepped into a horse's box and asked to have the rug removed. He took one quick look, and turned to the farmer and said, "Well, Mr. So and So, I am sure you must have bred this horse."

"Yes, as a matter of fact, I did," said the farmer, flattered. "How did you know that?"

"Because," Harold said, "I can't believe that even you would buy such an ugly bastard as this."

Another character, albeit of a different type, was Andrew McIlwaine, a most popular and charming man with an enviable philosophy. He always used to finish his letters to me and everyone with the expression, "Roll On," . . . which was part of a verse that typified the attitude that Andrew and his colleagues needed in this roller-coaster world of the dealer.

CHAPTER SIX

SILENT WEDDING

*It's no use crying over spilt milk
It only makes it salty for the cat.*

W. S. GILBERT

It should have been a very good day. I was about to marry the prettiest girl in Carlisle, it was 1920 and I had my own horse dealing business at last and I had more good friends than any one man ever had the right to expect.

But there was, alas, just one small thing which darkened my sky. I was lying on a hard bench in a police cell and nursing a broken jaw. It scarcely seemed a good omen for a wedding.

Yet the day had started pleasantly enough. I had met my fiancée, Ann Wood, in Newcastle and enjoyed a very relaxed evening. Then at ten-thirty, I had returned to the County Hotel and ordered a nightcap in the lounge. There were three other men at the bar, all big and somewhat belligerent. I was reading a paper when one of them came over and asked me to prove my identity. This all seemed a little odd, but I assumed he had some sort of authority. So I produced a letter. When this didn't satisfy him, I offered to fetch my bag from my room.

He said, "You don't think we're about to let you out of our sight, do you?"

Growing suspicious, I told him to go to hell. And at this, one of his companions attempted to seize hold of me. I stood up and knocked him down, the floor being slippery, which started a considerable free-for-all. I was eventually taken away to the local police station by these three men who turned out to be plain-clothes police officers. I was very literally thrown into a cell and, as I attempted to rise, kicked in the jaw.

The following morning, I appeared in court on some trumped-up charge, which was dismissed. My friends contacted a well-known lawyer called Strother-Stewart who started taking action against the Watch Committee. Needless to say, there was a terrible row in high places in Newcastle and headlines in the papers:

"Brutality by Police"
"Horse dealer awarded £500"
"Police scandal in Newcastle"
"Innocent man arrested and seriously maltreated"
"Members press for dismissal of all officers concerned"

Disciplinary action was eventually taken against the policemen involved. But, to summarise this very unfortunate affair, had I known these men were policemen, I would not, of course, have resisted them. What they really wanted, of course, was an excuse for the time they had squandered drinking in the County Hotel.

I was much more concerned with the effect this might have upon my forthcoming marriage. However, we were married the very next day by special licence though I could barely mutter, "I do."

Poor Ann! What a start to married life! I could have scarcely seemed the life and soul of the party. The jaw had been broken in two places and my teeth had to stay locked together. I had several operations and survived on a liquid diet, taken through a tube. Eventually the jaw healed, after nearly a year of misery.

My business naturally suffered too. Horse dealers can't afford to take breaks of this duration.

In 1920, after my marriage, I had bought a yard at Catterick, which was almost perfect for my purpose. It consisted of about twenty boxes with office, clipping box, coach house and manure pit, all very well architectured. The one fault which always troubled me was that the loose box doors opened inwards. A bad fault, because in the event of fire a horse would inevitably endeavour to suck clean air from under the door and whilst doing so would make it impossible to open the door from the outside. Also, horses could become "cast" in the door entrance. Happily there were no fires, but the problem was always uppermost in my mind.

I had one horse of whom I became very fond called Felix 11 . . . a good second-class 'chaser on whom I won races at Cartmel, Sedgefield and several point to points, one at the Cleveland in a snowstorm. No pedigree available, of course, but obviously thoroughbred. I have a lovely painting of Felix by George Paice and this shows the old poverty lines (beside Felix's tail) are very pronounced. He never put on weight. The vets treated him and we used the saline solution, but he never really improved in this respect. He was an odd customer, a very hard puller indeed and useless as a hunter. A cat was his constant companion and used to lay on his back for hours at a time.

When Charlie Mulholland arranged a post-mortem at his death, there was, I understand, a large cluster of worms present. Just think how much better a horse he would have been without these!

George Paice, the horse artist, used to come and stay with us, when he had portraits to do in the neighbourhood. We used to loan him a pony and trap and he would go off with his paints, brushes and canvasses. His work is still popular and, in many people's opinions, symmetrically perfect. This was the era when horses were usually painted in a loose box complete with straw together with the inevitable bucket, rug in the corner with owner's initials, and rack chain ring hanging from the wall. I still have several of his paintings which he always insisted upon leaving as payment for his bed and board.

Poor old George, I was very fond of him. His home was in London and he used to send cash home every week for his family. But the fees paid to him by horse owners were truly disgraceful, as little as £3 to £4. He was a very genuine artist and not given to flattering a horse. If a horse had a badly-shaped pair of hind legs, then that was the way they were portrayed.

I don't think he ever mentioned his age, but he must have been an old man, as I have in my possession his beautiful painting of Florizel 11 and that is dated 1901. (Lester Piggott lives in a house of that name in Newmarket.)

On the subject of horse artists, I remember the Alderson Sisters who painted in a combined fashion. One painting the fore and one the hind!

One of my first customers at Catterick was the Prince of Wales. I had bought a good, seasoned six-year-old hunter from a man I could trust in Ireland and he really was a patent safety. It occurred to me that the hunter would be ideal for the Prince who was then hunting with the Whaddon Chase. So I wrote to Fruity Metcalfe, who was his private secretary, suggesting this. I was told to bring two horses down.

Now the Whaddon was a very swagger affair and top hats were the dress of the day. I always wore a black coat and black bowler when hunting, and did so on this occasion . . . all of which led to an amusing incident.

Fruity, a rather impetuous sort of chap, took one look at the bowler and introduced me to the Prince as "Gibson's groom." He was a bit high and mighty about it too.

The Prince turned on him immediately. "That's not a groom," he snapped. "That's Gibson. We served together in Italy."

Poor old Fruity, whom I came to know well later, was most embarrassed. He came up to me afterwards and apologised.

He said, "I felt so terrible. I could have bitten my thumb off."

CHAPTER SEVEN

COCK OF THE NORTH

*The wheel that squeaks the loudest
Is the one that gets the grease.*

JOSH BILLINGS

Matthew Peacock stood beside the Manor House at Middleham, monarch of all he surveyed. His thick thumbs were pushed into the pockets of his waistcoat.

And sure enough, upon spotting a small boy coming back from the Hall Stable Yard, he roared in his best sergeant-major's voice, "And where are you going to?"

The boy, shifting his fork and the little tool sack upon his back, replied, "Please, Sir, I'm not going anywhere. I'm coming back." And with that, he walked on.

It was the only time in all the years I knew Matt Peacock that I can remember him totally lost for words. He really was a most dominating fellow and, when in the mood, could put fear into the hearts of brave men. He had indeed been a sergeant-major in the Yorkshire Hussars, and it showed.

When roused, his voice rebounded from one end of the stables to the other. But underneath this gruff exterior, he was really the kindest of men.

He feuded for years with fellow trainer, Dick Dawson. But when Dick fell on hard times, it was Matt who helped him out, while all his other so-called friends were busy looking the other way.

With his father, Dobson Peacock, he ran a stable that was

for long the pride of the North. He was a fine judge of both horses and men. And certainly Manor House couldn't have been better staffed. Yorky Waudby, the head lad, also rode successfully in National Hunt races. Harry "Swank" Smith was travelling head lad and the loyallest of the loyal. And so was the former head lad, Tommy Barnet.

I was down at the stables one day, when the news came through that Sir Ernest Tate, one of Matt's biggest owners, was coming down to have a look at his horses.

Tommy, with a fine touch of public relations, sprinkled fresh sawdust in odd corners of the boxes with a lot of puffing and blowing. He then inscribed Sir Ernest's initials in the sawdust and even produced buckets with "E.T." written large upon them. Even the most blasé owner couldn't fail to feel a little flattered at that.

The Peacocks were incredibly successful. In 1931, for instance, Dobson saddled 98 winners. And the following year, Matt went two better, training the magic hundred. Unlike the modern trainers, who can bolster their total with weekend visits to the Continent, the Peacocks only ran their horses in Britain.

Matt's long-time stable jockey was Billy Nevett, surely one of the most under-rated riders of the 1940s. I was very fond of Billy and always felt that his own modesty weighed heavily against him.

It was a flamboyant age and Billy was never a flamboyant man. This was borne out recently at Newmarket when, wanting a day's racing, he popped into the Jockey Club to collect his badge.

The people in the office didn't remember him and queried the request. I suppose, not having the buoyancy of Charlie Smirke or others I can think of, he didn't wish to remind them that he'd won four classics and been the top jockey in the North for two decades. Instead, he waited patiently and politely until the muddle was sorted out and accepted the apologies pleasantly enough. Alas! Worse was to follow. The gateman queried his ownership of the badge. Not Billy's day!

During his stay at Middleham, he was somewhat dominated by Matt Peacock. Weren't we all? But the Manor House set-up with the stable-jockey very much a part of the concern, telling the Guv'ner "the time of day" with the horses and riding for practically no one else was a sound affair.

I know the place very well, having fallen in love with Matt's step-sister Marjorie at a very early age. I used to ride my pony over from our home at Aysgarth to Middleham and would be told by Matthew, four times inside ten minutes, just where and when not to stable the pony.

Pattie Peacock would put Marjorie and me in the drawing room and we would hold hands for a few minutes, until tea was ready. Oh, for the long-lost days of my youth!

In later years when doing saddlery business with the Peacocks, I found it best to stand up to Matt. When he was in one of his warlike moods, I used to tell him that I knew perfectly well what he wanted and remind him that I had, after all, done it many times before to his satisfaction. He would then wilt a little and, after a couple of trips to the green cupboard in the kitchen, he would return and say, "Well, are you sure you won't have anything?" And, although this would probably be the first time he'd mentioned a drink, you nevertheless took the hint and departed. At least you did, if you were wise in the ways of Matt Peacock. The Peacocks were really most generous and many are the meals I had there.

He most certainly wasn't the easiest of men to handle, as the Armstrong family could testify. On one occasion, he was having some very strong words with one of the Armstrongs . . . something to do with the gallops on the moor, if my memory serves me.

And after some parting remark, he slammed the door of the Armstrong's car in fury. Alas, in so doing, his coat had become trapped in the hinge. As the car set off, he was dragged down the driveway, roaring like a lion.

Seemingly even Matt couldn't win them all.

CHAPTER EIGHT

AMERICAN INTERLUDE

One should produce a horse for sale
Keeping him balanced and looking good —
Display his virtues — conceal his faults
And pop him over the necessary fences
With apparent ease.

HOWARD MARSHALL

From the back of my horse, I could look out across the blue grass of Philadelphia to the horizon faraway. And in all that vast expanse of land, there wasn't a single house to trammel the skyline. I stepped down with a sense of well-being. I had just ridden an early-morning trial for my new boss, Sidney Holloway, and was confident that I had acquitted myself with credit. After all, I had come to America with a fairly good reputation as a nagsman.

I went back into the house and began shaving in preparation for my breakfast with the Holloways. His wife was a very striking woman with a touch of the Creole about her. She also had a voice which had something in common with that of Matt Peacock. Although rather more lilting, it carried just as far. So when she asked, "How did that new man perform out there?", I didn't miss a word.

I eavesdropped, ready to lap up the praise. I was more surprised than somewhat to hear Holloway say, "Bloody useless! He doesn't sit forward."

Even worse was to follow. After a rather strained atmosphere at the breakfast table, Holloway took me into his office and said, "I can't imagine what Harry Beeby was thinking about when he recommended you as an experienced rider. Didn't he warn you that you'd have to conform to the modern manner of the forward seat?"

Now, this was a comparatively new style of riding which had come into the States in a big way. I shrugged and told him, "No, I wasn't warned. But surely there's no harm done. I should be able to pick it up pretty quickly, particularly if you'll help me." At this, he became unexpectedly angry.

"I haven't got time to teach anybody" he said. Then nodding his head furiously, he added, "No, there's nothing else for it. You'll have to go."

I was becoming angry too and, hearing the rasied voices, "Boy" Bostwick came strolling into the office, carefree as ever.

"Is this a private fight?" he asked. "Or can anyone join in?"

Holloway wasn't amused. He said, "I've just told Gibson that he's of no use to me. He doesn't sit forward." He made this sound like the darkest sin. But Boy, good chap that he was, took my side instantly.

"Look, Sid," he said. "I've known Gibby for years. Give him a day or two to change to your ways and he'll be showing you all the way home."

A bit more persuasion followed and Holloway eventually relented. And I must say I did learn pretty quickly, as my future — and come to think of it, my existence too — depended upon it.

After that discouraging beginning, life on the Holloway ranch (for this is really what it was) moved along pleasantly enough. Holloway was an Englishman who had spent many years in the States and had consequently, become very Americanised. He was a splendid nagsman and quite able to tell you, if the occasion arose, to get down and he would perform himself. He could always think more clearly than the horse.

During my days at Berwyn, Philadelphia, I was fitter than I've ever been before or since. The work of riding the sale horses and showing horses was terribly strenuous. And in the hot weather, you couldn't ride a yard without a fly whisk. It was nothing to ride fifteen or more horses during Saturday and Sunday under a burning sun. And yet at that time it was exactly what I needed with long hard days and short dreamless nights. I had much that I wished to forget, as I'd made a hash of my life in England. My marriage had gone and my business too, and I suppose those two happenings were partly linked. It's very hard to explain, even to oneself, why two people should believe for a while that they were just made for each other. And then just a few years later, decide to depart. I've no doubt that the fault was largely mine. I was a very restless sort of fellow in those days, seemingly blown along by every wind.

I had, however, met someone to whom I became devoted and I was hoping for her to wait for me to make a few bob and return to England to marry her and this I did. Her name was Lilian Fenn and she has put up with me ever since and been a wonderful wife.

Berwyn was very different to anything I had known in England. The men, for instance, cleared off every evening and clocked in the following morning. There were a very large number of "boarders", what we term liveries in this country, and forty or fifty sale horses. There were kraals in which to school the horses and the trial field had to be seen to be believed. It had a vast number of fences over some of which the horses were ridden to impress the customers.

The establishment included farriers and a saddlers' shop, and every loose box had an automatic water bowl. There were also coconut-matting runners for special occasions together with lawns, trees and pleasant gardens.

At weekends, the rich and the powerful, used to come down to Berwyn. And along the paddock rails, we used to see a strange assortment of rich socialites. For this, remember, was the time of Prohibition and the angels and the sinners were on the same platform. The atmosphere was pure Scott Joplin and I must say I found it all very fascinating.

Many of the visitors seemed to find me fascinating too, albeit for a different reason. English accents, English clothes and certainly English saddles were all the rage in America at the time . . . and I, of course, had all three.

My clothes especially appeared to intrigue them all. I remember a millionaire from Boston saying to Holloway, "See your fellow has a pair of breeches, Sid. Where did he get them?"

The horses we rode were English too and mostly supplied by Harry Beeby. A few came from Bertram Mills and others from the Youngs. I also had visitors from England. Herbert Sutton, who later went as Horse Master to Major Sir Reginald Macdonald Buchanan, was a very welcome one. So too were the late "Goblin" Parker, a well-known professional nagsman, and Reg Hobbs, the father of Bruce who won the Grand National with Battleship in 1938. In those days, Reg was in charge of Ambrose Clarke's horses.

But, to me, the most interesting visitor to Berwyn was Elizabeth Altemus, one of the most beautiful women I ever knew and a quite superb rider. She was seemingly wooed by just about every eligible male in America and eventually settled down as Mrs. Jock Whitney.

But for me, at least, the party was over. America was on the brink of the Depression and the Wall Street crash was only weeks away. Sid Holloway just couldn't afford me any longer.

Another chapter in my life was over. I sailed home on *The Majestic*. I had a feeling that I was coming away from a doomed land.

CHAPTER NINE

BLACK DAY AT AINTREE

Behold — we put bits in horses mouths that they may obey us — we turn about their whole bodies.

ST. JAMES (Chapter II, Verse 3)

Jack Hance, riding master of Malvern and formerly my rough riding instructor in the Army, was standing in the centre of the ring, watching his pupils as they circled around him. Turning to me, he said, "Tell me, Gibby. In your opinion, which of those riders is most correctly positioned?"

I had already anticipated the question. I pointed to a man who seemed very much more part of the horse than anyone else. Not, I suspect, because he was the best horseman there that day, but because he had a saddle which helped him to blend with the natural movement of the horse. We examined his saddle and discovered that it was a broken-tread Bosca saddle from Australia. I took it away for repair and copied it, with one noted exception. I made the tree more like the broken one . . . in other words, more dipped.

Upon that very simple happening around 1931, the dipped saddle was born. I later modified it and made it with a spring tree. This then became known as the All Purpose saddle and was eventually to be copied by every saddle maker both in and out of London. But in reality, of course, very few things in life are literally born over night. I had been toying with the idea of a dipped saddle for years. And so too, I imagine, had Jack Hance.

The thought had first come to me in Philadelphia when riding over fences in a flat-seated English saddle. These gave me no security, so I knew that eventually dipped saddles would become popular. And then one day fate gave me the push I needed. The late Reg Hindley, captain of the Helsinki Olympic Games Team, father of the present successful young Newmarket trainer Jeremy, was one of the first to find these saddles a great help in keeping oneself in the desired position.

Like every new invention, they had their critics. I remember displaying one very prominently at the Olympia Horse Show and some ex-regular Service officer summoned his wife to come and see this extraordinary object.

"My God," he said. "What will they think of next?"

I asked him very quietly if he happened to have been a cavalryman. On hearing that he had, I asked why the saddle should seem so odd to him . . . seeing that every trooper sat in a very dipped saddle. He left, somewhat deflated.

I had first met Jack Hance during the First World War, when he had been a Rough Riding Bombardier at St. John's Wood Barracks. He had invited me to become part of a team of four who would put on a riding display to please the visiting "brass hats" from the War Office. My team mates were Robert Needham (later a partner in Tattersalls), Arthur Thompson (the horse dealer from Camberley), and "Boy" Hopkins, son of the well-known Cambridge dealer. All, unhappily, now dead.

In Jack's excellent book, *The Riding Master*, he refers to that eventful day at Malvern, but talks of a Mexican saddle, which is incorrect. It was a Bosca.

As you will have gathered, my life's course had again been changed by yet another puff of wind. On my return from America, I had seen an advertisement in the *Daily Telegraph* for a disinfectant salesman, which, frankly, didn't appeal very much. But it at least served as a stop-gap, until I could once more find my way back into that horsey world which I loved so much.

I eventually became a partner in this venture with a very

honest little man called Howard Asquith. And I don't imagine that it will surprise you too much to learn that, in addition to disinfectant, we were soon also selling such items as saddles, martingales and girths under the good supervision of a Walsall man called Joe Noake who was a first-class cutter. I was back among the horses. I had for a long time held various theories about saddlery and this gave me an opportunity to put some of these into practice.

One day, I called upon the late Joe Taylor and his brother Tom, well-known show-jumping enthusiasts at Warrington. Joe was finding some difficulty in choosing a suitable bridle for a potentially brilliant jumper. So I told him about my experiences with bitless bridles when with Sidney Holloway in America. He became so interested that I told our shop in London to send one to him straight away.

The bridle was what is known in the trade as having "Chifney action." Joe put Harold Holmes, his nagsman, up and the result was such a success that it caused something of a revolution in show-jumping circles.

Joe Taylor sold a couple of jumpers about this time to Lady Helen McCalmont and Mrs. "Binty" Marshall (mother of Bryan Marshall, the brilliant National Hunt jockey), and Lady Helen, I remember, had two of these odd bridles from us. So somewhere in County Tipperary, these may still be in some saddle room, though both ladies died some years ago. Mrs. Marshall was a formidable contestant in pre-war show-jumping contests at Olympia and Richmond, and rode side-saddle in all the events.

I had always wanted to exhibit my saddlery and perhaps discuss matters appertaining to the horse . . . different saddles and also particular bits and bitting. And I thought that, as someone who'd had a considerable amount to do with horses, I would be able to give assistance.

A new bit and some device is perhaps not so difficult to sell as it may appear. One reason can of course be that most animals respond to a new type of bit. And I wonder how many times a trainer has said to me how pleased he was with some certain bit . . . and I have hastened to say to him that if he is wise he will keep the bit for the race he wishes to win, before the animal becomes too familiar with it.

In 1936, we received some very unwelcome publicity, following the running of the Grand National. Among the extreme outsiders in the race, there was a horse called Davy Jones, a tubed reject from the flat. Lord Mildmay had bought him for £650, so that his son could have a ride in this, the most demanding of all steeplechases. At that time, Anthony Mildmay was an inexperienced amateur with an ugly style and no great ability. But Devon families were on him to a man, partly out of regard for his father, partly in admiration of his courage. A year before, he had been almost killed in the Foxhunters' Chase. That crashing fall might have been enough for most men, but long pain seemed only to make Anthony Mildmay more determined. The winning of the National had become his great dream.

We had supplied much of his saddlery to his trainer Peter Cazelet at Fairlawne and sometime before the race, he got us to shorten the reins. I counselled against this very strongly, but my advice wasn't taken.

It was a strong field, which included the winners of the two previous years, Golden Miller and Reynoldstown. But to everyone's surprise, certainly including mine, Davy Jones jumped into the lead on the first circuit soon after Valentine's and proceeded to run away from the rest of the field. He was a notorious puller and Mildmay was probably wise not to fight him for his head.

He was still leading over Becher's and as he came on to the racecourse, with just three fences left to jump, he was greeted by a huge Devonian roar. He seemed to be increasing the lead over the second-placed horse Reynoldstown with every stride.

He went on towards the second last and it was here that disaster struck. He jumped it well enough, but pecked slightly on landing. Mildmay allowed the reins to slip to the buckle, giving him space to recover. It was the correct thing to do and showed admirable coolness. But alas at that moment, the prong of the buckle slipped through the hasp and suddenly the reins were flapping. Mildmay lost control. Davy Jones swerved and ran out, scattering spectators who didn't know what had happened.

And amidst all the confusion, Reynoldstown ran on to win for the second successive year, a race which his connections had virtually given up for lost. At such moments of huge disappointment, people look around for someone to blame and the poor old saddler was an obvious target. Several of the reports in the following day's papers actually suggested that the equipment must have been at fault.

In fact, this most unfortunate happening had been brought about by two events:

1. The shortening of the reins.
2. Mildmay's failure to tie his usual knot in the end of the reins. If this had been there, they couldn't have slipped through his hands.

Two days after the race, I went down to see him at the Fairlawne Stables. I wanted to offer my sympathy and also to be quite sure in my own mind that the equipment couldn't have been to blame. If there was any doubt about this, I intended to make the necessary changes immediately . . . and so ensure that no other rider could suffer such a mishap with reins of mine. But Mildmay's trainer, Cazelet, still in a very emotional state, refused to see me. This was disappointing, but understandable.

On a more pleasant note, I had begun to give talks on saddlery to riding and pony clubs up and down the land. My first invitation came from Major Harry Faudel Phillips who ran the Temple Bar Riding Establishment. Now, Harry was a remarkable character and certainly one to take the eye. I remember Crystal Irvine, the very well-known veterinary surgeon of Shenley, looking at Harry with some astonishment and saying to me, "Gibby, who's that fellow over there who looks as though he's just had his dock sponged out?"

Harry was a fine showman and an exhibitor of show hunters up and down the country. There was a time when we North Countrymen were not too pleased to see him at shows such as the Great Yorkshire, as he had good show tactics and took the judges' eye pretty quickly.

He was one of those fellows who travel first-class through life. He even had a lady pilot, the efficient Dinah Heasman. But I will always remember Harry, with some gratitude, as the man who started me off on the lecture tours which I so enjoyed. You see, I was still following my father's dictum, by making my business my pleasure.

The world was coloured pink again.

CHAPTER TEN

THE MYSTERIOUS BAY

*Of all the recreations with which the heart be blessed
A chase amongst the mountains
Is the purest and the best.*

BLENCATHRA

The Officers' Mess at Aldershot was full of strangers, the proverbial ships that pass in the night. Aldershot at the beginning of the Second World War was such a transit town for the Army that you seldom had the chance or the time to make friends. At least I had one friend beside me that night, albeit a discontented one. Bay Parry was viewing the world through the bottom of a glass and not liking what he saw.

"You know, Gibby," he said. "You're a lucky begger. I'd give anything to be going out with you. Instead of that, I'll be stranded in this goddam awful place for the rest of the war, bored to tears."

This was typical of Bay who is perhaps better known to you as Dalesman of *Horse and Hound*. His whole life has been a series of adventures strung together . . . and he has no liking for the quiet days.

He served with the Seaforth Highlanders in the First World War, was wounded at Arras and has been lame ever since. But that seemingly only whetted the appetite of the man. He worked his passage round the world, languished in jail for murder, fought in the prize ring, was a swaggie in Australia, fought in a South American Revolution and was again badly wounded. In his spare time, as they say, he was a professional huntsman and also hunted the North Hereford, the Staintondale for twelve seasons and the United Shropshire where he kept a pack of Beagles for twenty years.

There had also been a rumour that he'd been the man who'd killed the murderer Percy Toplis, after a gun battle just outside Carlisle. I had always wanted to ask him whether this was true, but had hesitated. It is, after all, a delicate point to raise with even a friend. But this seemed as good a time as any to ask a question such as this. So I did.

He regarded me levelly for a long moment and then smiled, just a little.

Then he began to tell me the story, pausing every now and then to study some new arrival at the bar.

He said, "You probably remember the main details of the affair . . . how Toplis, a soldier at Bulford Camp, deserted, murdered a cabbie called George Spicer and drove off in his taxi, a silver-grey Daracq . . . and how despite a nationwide manhunt, Toplis remained at liberty for months, killing two more men and eventually winding up in Carlisle.

"Well, my father was Chief Constable of Cumberland and Westmorland at the time, and as soon as Toplis was spotted, I offered to help. I drove a motor bike along the road to Penrith, so that I could recognise him. I was being shadowed by a police car.

"And then sure enough, I passed this man in a brown suit, carrying a parcel. Glancing back over my shoulder, I saw the face that had been peering out of the wanted posters all over the land. He had shaved off his moustache and very tanned, due to his life in the open. But it was undoubtedly Toplis.

"I made a U-turn and came back towards him, raising my right arm as a signal to the police car. But as the car stopped alongside us, Toplis pulled out a gun and the civilian driver of the police car panicked and drove on . . . leaving me alone and backed up with an armed murderer."

Bay chuckled at the memory. "I've known better moments," he said. "The fellow was obviously mad and seemingly enjoying the situation. I told him to be a sensible chap and put the gun away, because he hadn't a chance. In no time at all, the area would be swarming with police. At this, he began to laugh.

"He said, 'I'll put the gun away, alright . . . after you're dead.' And with that, he fired at me and the bullet just missed my head. We were, I suppose, about fifteen yards apart, so this was pretty wild shooting. He incredibly missed with two more shots and these were ·45 bullets, which can make a big hole in a man.

"But all the time he was moving closer and he wouldn't have missed with the next. He was shot dead, before he could squeeze the trigger. He died instantly."

It had been a fascinating story. But Bay, who can be very Irish at times, had tantalisingly left the real question unanswered.

So I said, "Come on Bay. Tell me, were you the one who killed him?"

He paused and remained silent for so long that I didn't think he was going to answer at all. And then he shrugged, beginning to enjoy the situation.

"Put it this way," he said. "The police appeared to be under that impression. All the officers involved in the chase were given £25 a piece and silver watches. All they offered me was a prison cell. Among other things, I was accused of homicide, riding to the danger of the public and carrying a gun without a licence. You know, Gibby, it never paid to be honest."

Since then he had been Master of the United; was badly injured in the evacuation of Dunkirk, without honour; farmed in Cumberland and was Master of the Cumberland Hounds which was his life's ambition. He then purchased his old Inn, the Anchor, again. When sixty he established his own pack of hounds to hunt the hill country on the Welsh Border and became Joint MFH of the United with John Roberts. Having a bad fall he went back to his native Ireland to live on the Atlantic coast in County Mayo but spent the winters in County Cork and Kerry.

Now, in 1978, he has returned to Cumbria where he lives near Caldbeck.

CHAPTER ELEVEN

A FALLING STAR

Every good deed brings its own punishment.
LEO PARVA

Mouse Townsend was wining and dining me in Cairo . . . and fussing around like an old hen. Now this was unlike Mouse, normally the most forthright of men, and so I had an uneasy suspicion that I was about to be manoeuvred.

And sure enough round about the cigar stage, Mouse was saying, "Gibby, we've been friends a long time, haven't we?" I nodded.

"And I know that if it was in you power to help me out, you'd do so."

Again I nodded. There was no argument. I would gladly have helped Mouse at any time.

"In that case," said Mouse, suddenly rushing his words. "Will you take Basil Briscoe into one of your companies?" But Basil Briscoe, that was something else again.

Briscoe had been Golden Miller's trainer in the good days. But since parting from the formidable Dorothy Paget, he had fashioned a most unenviable reputation. He was trouble with a capital T and no sane-headed man wanted Briscoe under his command. Mouse had been reading my somewhat open mind.

He said, "You know, he's not all bad, Gibby. He's got some very nice qualities and he's always been wonderful with horses. You're really the last chance he's got. If he falls any further, there can be no hope for him."

I knew that Mouse and Briscoe both came from Cambridgeshire and that they'd once been friends. I also knew that if it meant this much to Mouse — to me, one of the greatest of all vets and a fine friend to boot — I just couldn't say no. He could have had the favour without the meal, but I didn't tell him that.

Still it was a very reluctant assent and I went to bed that night with a feeling that I would have reason to regret my decision.

It was 1941 and at that stage of the war, I was a major in command of a horse transport company in the French quarter of Beirut. And under me, I had a unique band of men, everyone an expert of some kind in the ways of the horse and the mule. The army had been combed to find them. There were saddlers, farriers, wheelwrights, jockeys, riding masters and the like.

My premonitions about Briscoe proved well founded. I had a signal that he was on his way to us from Haifa. The signal added that there had been a misunderstanding, to say the least, about the loss of a rifle — and that a charge would be made against him on arrival.

The last time I'd seen him had been in the winner's enclosure at Cheltenham and the change in the man was very noticeable. All the sense of assurance he'd shown that day had gone. And as he stood before my desk, he never once looked me in the eye. His attitude was a mixture of the hang-dog and the rebel.

I hadn't received an official report about the rifle and so I deliberately didn't mention it.

I was most anxious that he should have the chance to settle in happily. He was a private and everyone else on the base was either a non-commissioned or commissioned officer. So I told him I was promoting him to corporal and putting him in charge of feeding the depot horses.

I said, "With your experience, you can be a big help to me here."

For the first time, he looked straight at me.

"I'll certainly try," he said.

"So will I," I promised.

And I did too. I never tried harder to put a man back on to his feet. Despite all the stories I'd heard, I still felt desperately sorry for him. Yet with the wisdom of hindsight, I realise now that I was embarking upon an impossible task. Basil Briscoe didn't wish to be helped.

He'd started out with every chance in life. Eton, Cambridge, a rich father and a considerable talent too. For there can be no doubt that he had great gifts as a trainer. But he had this self-destructive bent.

In the space of a few brief years, he had fallen a long, long way. He wished to continue falling. He made himself unpopular with the men, deliberately so I believe. He pushed the most patient of sergeant-majors to the brink of despair. And he was a constant irritation to me too. But perhaps for Mouse's sake, perhaps for my own (I hate to be beaten), I kept on trying.

I used to encourage him to talk about the old days, which in his case weren't that old, and I did become very intrigued by his relationship with Dorothy Paget . . . the key, of course, to both his rise and fall. It seemed something of a love-hate affair.

He said to me once, "She used to be very beautiful, you know, before she started wearing those frumpy clothes. And when I started, she was the best loser you ever saw. She became impossible. No man could work for her. Sometimes I wish I'd never met her."

But without doubt, the real love of his life was Golden Miller whom he originally bought for £500. I asked him what qualities about this great 'chaser had first impressed him and again he surprised me.

"None," he said. "I bought him unseen and didn't like the look of him at all. He seemed so big and ungainly, like a cart-horse. If I could, I'd have sent him straight back. He was hopeless as a hunter too, absolutely useless. And then one day, I saw him really turn it on at Newbury. He didn't jump. He just seemed to float over his fences. I knew then that I had something very special. From then on, my life was wrapped around him. For the seven years he was with me, I never once took a holiday. That's how much he meant to me."

The phone call from Dorothy Paget, which changed her life and his, came when she first decided to go into racing. She asked him whether he had any good horses.

"Oh, yes," he said. "I've got the best 'chaser in the world and the best hurdler in England."

He proved that very remarkable boast very convincingly during the following fifteen months by twice taking the Cheltenham Double (Gold Cup and Champion Hurdle) with Golden Miller and Insurance.

If 1934, when The Miller won both Gold Cup and Grand National, was the year of triumph for Briscoe, the following one had to be the one of disaster. For after winning the Gold Cup again, Golden Miller failed dismally at Aintree. Showing no liking at all for that awesome course, he made little apparent effort and popped Gerry Wilson out of the saddle at the open ditch after Valentine's. A few days later, Miss Paget removed all her horses from Briscoe's yard.

I asked him why he thought she'd taken this very drastic action and for once all the vagueness slipped away.

"Because her pride had been hurt," he said. "Golden Miller had given her a popularity she could never have found any place else. He had become the idol of the crowds and so had she. At Aintree in 1935, they'd all come to see The Miller. The women were wearing golden caps and the Prince of Wales had made a special journey to be there.

"Then when he failed, you could hear the booing all the way down the course. But they weren't booing me. They weren't booing Gerry Wilson and they certainly weren't booing the horse. They were booing the owner . . . and she knew it. I saw her just after the race and she was white-faced and shaking.

"She had pushed the horse too hard. No one should expect a horse to go for that sort of Double two years in a row. After he'd won in '34, we knew he didn't like the course. I advised against running him there again, but I was over-ruled."

It was one of the few times I saw him show any real emotion. And it went away as suddenly as it had arrived. And he concluded very tamely, "You see, she couldn't forgive me for being right, when she was wrong. I didn't watch when they came to take The Miller away. There was no point. It was all over."

Sadly it was. Basil Briscoe, that bright young star of the Thirties, never returned to racing. For him, seemingly, that palmy past was beyond redemption.

CHAPTER TWELVE

DESERT COMMAND

*Anyone remaining calm in this confusion
Simply does not understand the situation.*

R. C. DEBENHAM

I suppose only the British Army would have made Mountjoy Fane a Company Commander. But then maybe only the British would have appreciated the true qualities of this most unusual man.

For much of the time, he lived in a Bertie Wooster world, stumbling (sometimes rushing) from one misadventure to another. The most strange and wondrous things were always happening to Mountjoy. Yet when it mattered most, when the chips were down, he could be cool, decisive, even brilliant and a good man to have on your side.

We had first met during our days in North Yorkshire where our mutual love for the horse had drawn us together. We met again in Aldershot at a time when the Germans were sweeping all before them. France had fallen and the Allies were being pushed back into the Mediterranean. But if this depressed Mountjoy, it didn't show.

I was much older than my fellow officers, who all looked to me like pink-faced boys. They were well-meaning and pleasant enough, but their ways weren't my ways any more. And when you reach that stage in life, you know that your own youth has gone beyond recall.

Towards the close of a pleasantly nostalgic evening, Mountjoy said, "Oh, by the way Gibby, I'm off to Crete in a few weeks' time. I'd like to have you with me."

And that was how it all began. It ended with me in command of a horse-transport unit which stretched right through Syria, Palestine and into the Lebanon. It was almost certainly an historic command, for it seems very unlikely that horses will ever be used on this scale again in a major war. But how useful! In the Lebanon, we were moving about 28,000 tons of vital war supplies per week and a further 15 to 20,000 in Syria and Palestine.

I was fortunate to have a unique corps of men, all experts in their own branch of the horsey world. I was doubly fortunate to have two men, Hugh Delmege from Tipperary and Leslie Weaver, who were both aides and friends.

Although we had been with horses all our lives, there was still much to learn in a different land. For instance, when Hugh and I were first introduced to the forage which was called "tibbin", we were most unimpressed. But in fact it was superb, being barley straw, broken up by what one could call a wood harrow and really similar to "flakes".

The only problem was that the contractors had a habit of leaving sand in the tibbin, which gave the horses sand colic. So when Sandy Watney came to me, I suggested that as a brewer he would know something about barrels and vats. He did and we found it was just as easy to feed the tibbin wet (with barley), so we washed it in water vats and the sand sank to the bottom, thus saving a lot of trouble.

The stables in Beirut, Damascus, Homs and Aleppo were well built and, as the French had used their horses in three, the stalls were also designed for threes. However, we decided to use two horses to a waggon and each waggon was fitted for one or two poles. With over two thousand horses in my command, I had a shortage of horse-drawn vehicles. So we improvised.

We arranged with the Ordnance Corps to alter discarded three-ton lorries (minus engine) into waggons by making a full lock turntable in front to which a metal pole was inserted, leaving the braking system in working order. The crown wheel was turned parallel to the ground and we fixed solid tyred wheels which had been taken off Italian tanks. The results were excellent.

Our vets were absolutely first-class and all well-known in racing circles. Mouse Townsend was the senior veterinary officer and we travelled thousands of miles together, visiting units. I had more in common with Mouse than with his fellow officers, Ernest Peatt and Glyn Lloyd who were more "administration" and less "vet" minded.

On one occasion in Tripoli, a young vet had decided to have a horse destroyed. I arrived to find the Arab driver, waving his arms about and trying to explain in very basic English that there was basically nothing wrong with his horse. The vet was in no mood to listen. I knew the horse well. He was a "shiverer" and couldn't "back" a load. It was for this reason that I had transferred him from a single cart and given him a partner. The other horse was thus able to do all that was necessary when backing.

Once having got a pair to work satisfactorily together, we were loath to part them. So I countermanded the order, whereupon the young vet appealed to his superiors. Glyn Lloyd was a little upset about the incident, but with Mouse it would have been a "joke".

Still, I could understand people such as Frank Cundell and Bob Crowhurst being somewhat bored in helping me keep some very aged French semi-cart horses and old Yeomanry horses going when they had been used to dealing with valuable thoroughbred animals. Sometimes they would say, "Well, Gibby, I think we had better shoot him," knowing full well that Remounts had plenty more to send me.

Mouse was always full of interesting anecdotes and told me the story of the farmer upon whose hunter he had just operated for his wind. Mouse assured him that the horse would be in fine fettle in no time at all . . . as good as ever, except that he wouldn't be able to neigh. Upon this, the farmer asked him how much he would charge to operate on his "old woman."

As time went by, I saw less and less of Mountjoy and I viewed this with mixed feelings. Although he had enlivened my days, he had alarmed me too. It was all too easy to become involved in those Wooster-like adventures. During our initial voyage to the Middle East, he purchased a monkey on the quayside at Freetown and installed it in his cabin. He (Mountjoy) had been celebrating rather freely, which perhaps explains why he forgot to mention this new acquisition to his cabin companion. It scared the poor fellow half to death.

On another occasion Major-General Goldney sent Mountjoy and I to a camp near Haifa called El Mansura to command (if we could!) a holding company of a varied number of Cypriots. The number was unidentifiable, because they deserted and returned more or less at will. Well, we set off and, like all Mountjoy's operations, it was certain to be out of the ordinary. Almost before our train had begun to move, he was proposing a change of plan.

"It's quite clear to me, Gibby," he said. "That these fellers at HQ have given us the wrong location. The damn place is near Ramle not Haifa."

This seemed highly unlikely to me and I suggested that we would be much wiser to follow our original instructions and push on to Haifa. But Mountjoy wouldn't be budged. Ramle it had to be. Of course, there should have been a very simple solution to our problem. We had a map reference. Alas, we didn't have a map. Mountjoy had somehow mislaid it along the way.

So we stepped down from the train in the middle of nowhere. And after some trekking across the desert sand, we reached a camp and discovered that there was indeed an El Mansura near Ramle. The only trouble being that it was the wrong one. Palestine is seemingly filled with El Mansuras.

The following day, we rejoined the train and went to Haifa, where I had begged him to let us go in the first place. Maybe we'd have been wiser to have stayed at Ramle, after all. We took over the Cypriot Company from a major and a few officers who were delighted to see us. They just couldn't get themselves off to the Italian front quickly enough. And Mountjoy and I soon began to understand why.

We had hundreds of very unpredictable Cypriots under our command, thoroughly bored and bent on causing real trouble. Let me say that I was confident these men would, and did, behave very bravely when leading mules up the hills and into the line. But when unemployed and amongst civilians, they were extremely difficult to control.

After a week or so in El Mansura, we had begun to get the situation under control and then Mountjoy had another of his misadventures. It was pay day and I was just about to set off for Haifa to draw the money from the Paymaster when Mountjoy made yet another change of plan.

"Don't worry, Gibby old boy," he said. "I'm going to town anyway to visit the Club. So I'll pick up the cash for you."

At two o'clock, the pay lines formed up and I was still waiting somewhat anxiously for the money, when Mountjoy appeared.

"Sorry, old boy," he said. "I've had a bit of a mishap. I've lost the money, every single penny."

Apparently he had returned from Haifa with the money in a tin box and, on arrival back at camp, had locked it securely and placed it beneath his bed. Returning after lunch he found that the "boys" had got hold of the box and opened it by some means or another and the money was gone. In that sort of company, leaving anything about was courting disaster. Just about anything movable was apt to disappear.

Mutinies have been sparked off by lesser affairs than the loss of men's pay. However, by dint of a lot of swift talking, I managed to calm things down.

By and large, it wasn't too bad a war for me. Certainly preferable to the mud of Flanders. And I found the Lebanon in particular the most beautiful country. When I was about to leave, I went to see a noted art dealer and told him that I wanted a picture of the country. He replied that no artist had ever managed to capture the scenery behind the city, the mountains, the snow and so on. And I did see what he meant, because it does change hourly. Snow stays up in the hills, supplying water until around September.

One could comfortably bathe on Christmas Day and then go into the hills near the Cedars and ski the same day. I have often had the urge to return to that pleasant land. But life has taught me that it isn't always wise to return to a place where you have been more or less happy in the past. Old towns, like old loves, are sometimes best left in the memory.

When the war finally ended, I kept my own riding animals and a four-in-hand team. This team was particularly easy to handle, because it had the most perfect near-side "leader" (right-hand traffic), a wall-eyed bay, a charger from the Cheshire Yeomanry, who kept dead straight regardless of shouting crowds, trams, buses, the lot. And remember these horses didn't wear blinkers. The bridles were plain. In addition being long-tailed, one did get a bit of "rein under tail" trouble. But an active Arab lad would be riding behind, ready to run along and free your rein.

The only sad thing about the coming of peace was that the vast majority of the horses under my command were subsequently shot and sold as horsemeat. This does seem the final indignity to heap on a noble and courageous animal.

As always, it proved rather more difficult to get out of the army than in and demob arrangements did drag on interminably. Finally in Boulogne, I gave fate a bit of a push. Without waiting for my demob papers, I walked on to a ship bound for home. I did hear my name being called over the loudspeaker, but deemed it wise to lay low. And that, for me, was the end of my second war.

CHAPTER THIRTEEN

ANGEL ON HORSEBACK

The lift of his action is rhythmic and right,
His depth through the heart is a horseman's delight.
His tail flows to earth like the falls of the Clyde,
The arch of his crest is the badge of his pride.

ANON

Angel Peralta was in the bar at the Hyde Park Hotel, dominating the stage, as always, without even trying.

"Of all sports," he said, "only bullfighting and motor racing really try a man. All the rest are mere receations, games that children can play."

This is the doctrine by which Peralta lives. No man was ever more in love with danger. He is an avowed romantic and it has been remarked that in another era, he would have been a Crusader, or a knight-errant.

He often dressed totally in black. His hair was black too, usually long over his ears and neck. I first met him at the Horse of the Year Show at Wembley in 1960 and came to know him well in the years that followed. I found him utterly charming or utterly frightening, according to his moods. Sometimes, in repose, he has the look of a hired killer, but more often he resembles a Spanish grandee . . . which conveniently enough, is what he is.

His friends will tell you that he was born three or four centuries too late.

"Every time I see Angel," one of them told me, "I see him in a long cape, a sword sticking out of it, a floppy black hat on his head, riding like a fiend across some castle drawbridge."

His range of talents is awesome. In addition to having been the greatest bullfighter of his day (some would say, of all days), he has been a poet for his own satisfaction, jai-alai player and one of the finest natural horsemen I've had the pleasure to watch.

At Wembley, with his wonderful old horse Nightingale, he stole everyone's thunder. As his signature tune, Espana Cani, The Stripper, was played, horsemen from all over the arena would come down to the rails to watch. The highlight of the act came when Nightingale would stand, balanced on one hind leg. A most incredible sight.

Peralta's mastery of the horse was essential to him. His life depended upon it. He was a great exponent of Rejoneo (bull-fighting on horse-back) where the slightest misunderstanding between horse and rider could be fatal.

On certain occasions Peralta, after performing a dressage act, would come before the Royal Box, remove his hat and then canter backwards to the exit. This, I believe, was done without using the reins.

Naturally enough, with a man who hunted danger the way Peralta did, there had to be accusations of a death-wish. I once asked him whether this was so.

"A lot of nonsense," he said. "I don't think anyone enjoys fear. You can enjoy courage . . . the performance of an act which frightens you . . . but not fear.

"It may sound strange, but I think that because bullfighters are very close to death, they are more sensitive to life and appreciate it more. I'm sure I love life more than the average man does. I want to get something out of every minute. I want no time wasted.

"I want to live to be one hundred and five, and I mean to. I want to live to be a very old man. I'm enchanted with life. But no matter how long I live, I still won't have time for all the things I want to do."

His belief in his own immortality wasn't always echoed by his friends. His agent, Pepe Forbes, a friend of mine, who made our conversation possible — Peralta's English is frequently hard to understand — had grave doubts.

He told me, "I know Peralta says he'll live forever, but sometimes he scares me half to death. He takes such chances."

Quite apart from Peralta's personality, I was fascinated by his dressage skills . . . a subject which has always interested me. Around 1935, a customer of mine, Mrs. Dorothy Morton of Brampton Ash near Market Harborough, invited Henri Cuyer to her place to run a school. And this was really the start of dressage in Britain.

Dorothy Morton's sister Lorna Johnstone took to dressage about this time. They are the daughters of Major Wales-Fairbarn of Askham Grange near York. Both are talented. Dorothy paints and has exhibitions in various chateaux in France. She has also played various instruments for the BBC and Lorna is well known in the dressage world today . . . and has, incidentally, been most helpful in keeping me straight in this chapter.

Cuyer's devoted pupils were surprised and somewhat horrified that he should agree to join Bertram Mill's Circus to give a performance. The exaggerated "aids" seen at the circus apparently offends the true dressage enthusiast.

But Cuyer told Lorna, "You have to make things look difficult in the circus to impress an ignorant public, whereas the art of dressage is to make everything look easy."

A year later, Alphonse Kossmayer, an Austrian, brought over to Olympia a good-looking liver-coloured chestnut horse called Champagne. Alphonse entered the ring wearing a pink swallow-tail coat, top hat and black riding trousers and cantered extremely slowly once round. It was one of the most beautiful sights as Alphonse was an elegant horseman — tall, slim and never moved a muscle. It has been explained to me very kindly by Mary Phillips that this performance needed an enormous amount of collection and to know what to do with the collection when you had got it. It was not a "gimmick" but a wonderful movement with rider and horse in perfect unison.

Wenzel Kossmayer, Alphonse's cousin, then paired up and they did a high school act together. Later each came into the arena and carried out different movements separately — Wenzel riding a grey horse called Killarney.

For some years Mills put on an act called the "Cosmaries" — consisting of the Kossmayers and Mary Sykes and Mary Dee — the ladies having been schooled by the Kossmayers. Later Mary Sykes had instruction from Henri Cuyer in this country and at Neuilly in France. Later still, Mary married Tom Phillips, now a Stud Manager, and she won many point-to-points showing great versatility.

After the war Lorna arranged for Henri Cuyer to take courses at John Tilke's establishment near Stratford-on-Avon and these took place annually for a number of years. Eventually, Cuyer (who suffered from bronchitis and always feared he would become ill and be unable to carry out his commitment) decided it was too great a strain and declined to take further courses. He did, however, come over for a week each summer to assist Lorna and she kept in touch with him till 1970 when he died aged 82.

Mary Sykes had two sisters, Nan and Joan, who were just about the best people around with ponies at one time. The two sisters were given great help by Johnnie Moss, well known in the show ring today. Their father Jack Sykes, originally a harness horse man, started to deal in hunters and I used to meet him at the horse auctions. He became a good friend of mine. Jack bought middle class "cut and come again" types for a number of North Country hunting men and lived in Cheshire where he was very popular. Unfortunately he died a comparatively young man. Nan, through her excellent management and good judgment at a school at Frimley, cleared all her father's outstanding liabilities, helped by the fact that when a man like that dies sometimes a lot of debts are conveniently forgotten by debtors.

CHAPTER FOURTEEN

CASTLES IN SPAIN

We are the music makers,
We are the dreamers of dreams,
Wandering by lone sea-breakers,
And sitting by desolate streams;
World-losers and world-forsakers,
On whom the pale moon gleams:
We are the movers and shakers
Of the world for ever, it seems.

A. W. E. O'SHAUGHNESSY

The house in Bloomsbury had seen better days and so too, it must be admitted, had its occupants. The rooms had been let off as bed-sitters for the old and the lonely, and the derelicts too. In that setting, Count Ilias Toptani looked like a diamond in a cluster of glass. He was a big, swashbuckling sort of fellow with very white teeth and oceans of style.

He took me by the hand and said, "Gibson, my dear fellow, I must congratulate you. That dipped saddle of yours is the best thing I've seen since I came to England . . . made by a fellow horseman I can tell."

He smiled and I could feel the force of the man. It was a tangible thing. "We're going to do great things together," he said . . . and somehow I didn't doubt him for a single moment.

Toptani was apt to have that effect upon people. He was a mover and a shaker, a believer of such intensity that his faith was contagious.

I did, of course, know a little bit about him before that first meeting in 1952. He was an Albanian and a cousin of King Zog. He had been living in the Argentine and was regarded as one of the world's leading show-jumpers.

He explained that he wished to make certain modifications to my saddle, so that it would fit the specific needs of the show-jumper. My All Purpose Saddle had been designed for use also in dressage, hunting, hacking, ordinary riding and so on. I liked his ideas and, caught up in his enthusiasm, spent the next fourteen days almost entirely in his company. We visited tree makers and the makers of stirrup-leather bars and through the good offices of my friends, the Beebee Brothers of Walsall, soon found a tree which pleased him. It had one great innovation, namely the sinking of the bar by placing of the bar beneath the tree . . . thus avoiding any discomfort to the thick part of the leg. We had these saddles produced and started to sell them quite successfully.

At this time I was working as salesman to George Parker & Sons Limited of St. Martin's Lane and the success of the Toptani Saddle caused me to leave the good old firm because we could not agree on the commission resulting in the saddle's success.

This rift caused me to start my own firm — but not as maker of the Toptani saddle. I had overnight acquired a new partner and one very much to my liking. He was such a dreamer of dreams that it was impossible not to grow fond of him. He was also the most amusing fellow imaginable.

One day to my surprise, he arrived dressed as the typical city businessman, with brief-case, bowler and rolled umbrella. He explained that he'd just bought them in a lost property sale. I asked him why and he said, "Because I want to look like an Englishman," and with that, he began to wave his arms about in a very Latin way indeed.

His finances, rather like mine at the time, were at a low ebb. he had a lot of money tied up in the Argentine due to a dispute he'd had with the Peron Government. But he had developed a talent for living very well on very little.

He had, for instance, found an Italian restaurant in Soho and a waitress who had fallen beneath the Toptani spell . . . women were always apt to do that. And this waitress used to woo him with extra large helpings of spaghetti bolognese. You had to be prepared for almost anything when you went dining with Toptani. He was always liable to reach out in the most absent-minded way and slap the bottom of some pretty waitress, as she walked by. The odd thing was that very few of them ever seemed to mind.

On one occasion, I had taken him out to dine in a Hungarian restaurant and was a little shaken by the size of the bill. He must have seen the pain in my eyes. He plucked it from my nerveless fingers, whistled through his teeth as he read it and summoned the manager with an imperial wave of the hand. For someone who had barely two shillings to rub together, he could be remarkably imperial when he so wished. The manager, a fierce-looking fellow with a Zapata-type moustache, arrived to be harangued in fluent Hungarian. Toptani seemed to speak every language like the mother tongue.

Halfway through a sentence, he reached for my wallet, extracted enough notes to pay for half the bill, pushed them into the top pocket of the manager, told him he was damn lucky to get that much, then rose with some dignity and walked towards the door. I followed hastily, aware of the fact that the manager was padding along behind me in what I considered a most menacing manner.

Even then, Toptani couldn't resist the dramatic exit. There was a cigar stand just inside the door. He took a Havana, announced airily that this was his commission for bringing me there and then stepped out into the night.

He used to embarrass me terribly at times by his down-to-earth methods of selling a saddle. He would tell the prospective purchasers seated in the saddle on a dummy horse to push their bottoms in. And he was by no means averse to giving them a firm slap. I noted that most of the ones he slapped were pretty.

But the day I did admire his salesmanship was that on which we visited the British equestrian team at Porlock before the Helsinki Olympics of 1952. For both of us, this was very much the ultimate test. If we could sell them to the Olympic team, we could sell them to anyone.

But show-jumpers of the quality of Harry Llewellyn, Wilf White and company obviously have very definite ideas about saddles, which are unlikely to change in an instant. And so it seemed. They studied them and listened to what we had to say with the utmost courtesy. But I could tell that they weren't really too impressed. Toptani knew it too.

He had a brief word in German with Weetzen the German dressage expert brought over to teach the team dressage. Then he slipped one of the new saddles on to a horse, stepped up in one flowing movement and proceeded to ride it round the course with his arms folded when actually negotiating the obstacles. He rode with the reins till he jumped the fences. He made it appear the easiest thing in all the world. And even riders of this ilk had to be impressed with this brand of showmanship.

Once again, he couldn't resist hamming it up a little. Upon stepping down, he said very casually, "Of course it's up to you entirely. But personally I think you'd be damn fools if you don't take them." And so saying, he walked away.

The sale had been made. The saddles went to Helsinki and played their part in Britain's winning of the gold medal. Perhaps it was a sign from above. From that moment on, the fortunes of Toptani, whom I always knew as Ali, began to improve. His money arrived from the Argentine. He went to live in Spain and, in no time at all, I received a letter from Avila, saying that he had just married the Duchess of Valencia . . . and when were we coming to see them?

In fact, my wife and I went that very summer and I was delighted to see that fortune had indeed smiled on my old friend. His new home, the Palazzio, was a far cry from that bedsitter in Bloomsbury where we'd first met.

The Palazzio was feudal, had rooms galore, with beautiful pictures, libraries, four-poster beds and a private chapel. There were also some magnificent horses and a garden of rare charm.

Toptani hadn't changed at all. At supper one night, he had invited a Catholic priest, together with four people of Italian and Spanish nationality . . . and all of us only speaking our own language.

Yet he kept the party going very pleasantly, talking to us all in turn, and at the same time playing chess with the priest on a miniature board. He beat him too.

He looked just about as content as a man can be.

CHAPTER FIFTEEN

HAT FOR A HORSE

*At every show where horses are
In every county near and far
You'll find him throned beneath a sign
GIBBY — PASTMASTER at shooting a line!
If you're an old hunting man who likes to sit,
On a horse's weakest anatomical bit,
BE PREPARED! He'll pity, cajole, might even get shirty,
But before you walk out you'll have bought a "630".
If you want your horse to stand on his head,
Or to wield a fork and make his own bed,
To gallop smartly in reverse,
Or even to neigh in iambic verse,
With the mien of a Bishop and a cheek all his,
With never a smile on that foxy phiz,
He'll say, "Course it really 'ain't new
I made one for Blank in nineteen-o-two".
Names of the great in the world of the Horse,
He knows them all as a matter of course,
He's made them saddles, bridles and whips,
Given them all some useful tips.
Lords of the menage, Kings of the show,
All with reverence to Gibby go.
BECAUSE — and this is his 'tour-de-force',
Not GOD but GIBBY invented the HORSE!*

ELWYN HARTLEY-EDWARDS

In the summer of 1957, I elected to step into the world of high fashion on behalf of my four-footed friends. I decided to revive the vogue for the straw horse bonnet. And by kind permission of *The Times*, this chapter is reprinted from a leading article of the day, which appealed to me greatly:

The Times, Thursday June 13 1975.

A HORSE IN A HAT

A Newmarket saddler is of the opinion that women riders like to see hats on their horses' heads, and to back his judgment he has asked Luton manufacturers to make two dozen straw hats for them — for the horses, that is, not the riders. The hats are to be of Spanish design with a small conical centre with room for him to cut holes in the side for the horses' ears, an ensemble which would seem to combine elegance and comfort. No doubt the saddler knows best, but, even so, the proceeding must strike the impartial observer as not without its dangers.

With high summer and the Season approaching, women, when it comes to hats, are likely to find enough competition from their own kind without having to fear a flank attack from their four-footed friends. It would be intolerable to bear off the crown at Ascot with some incredible creation perched precariously on the back of the head only to be outdone by some flighty young filly from France with a bonnet saucily hung over one large equine ear. The business of horses is to win races on the racecourse, not to triumph in the fields of millinery.

Nevertheless, there is something pleasant and endearing about a horse in a hat, something that reaches back into a past not so far away in the actual number of years but, in all other respects, remote. In the days when a traffic jam meant a conglomeration of horse-drawn, and not petrol-driven, vehicles, memory insists that quite a number of horses in the summer months sported a variety of straw boater, although at this distance of time it would be imprudent to guess whether the design was, or was not, Spanish.

At any rate, the sight of a crowd of horses, divided as to the wearing of hats roughly in the same proportion that men are today, drinking with a kind of slow, thankful solemnity at one of London's many horse troughs, fits in with the general picture of London's past, with the street cries that are no more, with the tinkle of the muffin-man's bell, now forever silent.

The Newmarket saddler, in other words, will be reviving an old fashion rather than initiating a new one, but the scheme, considered as a whole, is pleasing.

CHAPTER SIXTEEN

PRINCESS ON THE RUN

*There is much to happen
Twixt the stirrup and the ground.*

ANON

It was one of those peaceful moments at Badminton that sometimes follow the rain. The sun was shining through the still wet trees and people, spirits rising, were moving slowly, speaking gentle. And then all of a sudden, I spotted Princess Margaret running towards me and I knew that the peaceful interlude was over.

Princesses very seldom run in public and so there had to be a good reason. The good reason was all too apparent. Tony Armstrong-Jones was running beside her. And a hundred yards away, but gaining rapidly, there was a photographer. It was the very early stage of the young couple's romance and they were seemingly considered fair game by the press of the world.

The Princess halted beside me, saying breathlessly, "I must get away." And then before I could answer, she fled through to the back of the stand where, alas, there was no way out.

In the distance I could see other photographers advancing. Armstrong-Jones was understandably angry and growing more so by the moment. It had all the ingredients of the kind of incident which can make the wrong sort of headlines. So without too much time for thinking, I shepherded them into the caravan which formed the back of the stand, and stepped out again just in time to see the first photographer arrive.

"Have you seen the Princess?" he said.

Very innocent of eye, I asked, "Which princess would that be?"

A few minutes later, after the search had moved on by, I returned to the caravan and, with Armstrong-Jones' help, opened a little-used door at the back through which they fled like thieves in the night.

In fact, we became quite accustomed to visits from the Royal Family. The Duke of Beaufort, who used to be most friendly and helpful to our firm, brought Her Majesty Queen Elizabeth to our stand on several occasions. And it was a great pleasure explaining the finer points of saddlery to her, as she was obviously so interested. If she has one over-riding passion in life, it is surely for the horse . . . and certainly she is very knowledgeable.

I always prided myself upon being something of a trailblazer in the saddlery world. And if there was the slightest innovation on the stand, she would spot it instantly and ask to have it explained to her in detail.

My friend Harry Carr who was the royal jockey during two reigns once told me a very revealing story about the Queen. When staying at Sandringham, she was apt to visit her horses at early morning exercise.

On one occasion when Harry stepped down, she said, "Didn't I see your horse change his legs?"

"Yes, that's right," said Harry surprised.

"Just about a furlong out," she said. And Harry agreed again.

He told me, "It was just a momentary change of action. At that distance very few professionals would have spotted it."

On another and earlier occasion Harry (in the royal colours) rode a very close finish against the Australian Rae Johnstone at Ascot. As they entered the winner's enclosure neither knew who'd won. They didn't even see the result go up in the frame. But Harry suddenly saw the Queen (Princess Elizabeth as she was then) jumping up and down with joy.

He says, "Then I knew for the first time that we'd won."

I suppose I was really the first saddler to see the possibilities in attending sales, and shows, and events. And I will always be grateful to the organisers of the One- and Three-Day Event venues such as Badminton and Burghley for helping to make this possible. I know several of them had grave misgivings when I first mooted the idea. But they were fair and open-minded men, prepared to listen. I pointed out that such stands would supply a very real service to the riders who could so easily break a stirrup leather or need some vital piece of equipment at a moment's notice. I also pointed out that spectators would take pleasure in viewing the very latest trappings from the world of the horse.

Upon that argument, the notion was born. I was speaking a language common to us all.

CHAPTER SEVENTEEN

OLD PALS OF MINE

Come fair or foul or rain or shine
The joys I have possessed in spite of fate are mine
Not Heaven itself upon the past has power
But what has been has been, I have had my hour.

DRYDEN

Now that I move towards the close of my story, I become aware of the friends I've left out along the way. The reason for their omission, their sole sin, was that they failed to herald some great new adventure, some new turning point, some new direction in my life, the stuff of which autobiographies are made.

They didn't push me towards either the valley or the mountain top. But nevertheless they did enrich my life. Just by being there. And I remember them more vividly then some of the more famous names who have already faded into the backrooms of my mind.

I can see, as though it was yesterday, John Smith-Maxwell standing in front of his open hearth, smiling, a glass in his hand, the prince of good fellows. An original man with an original vocabulary. Money was "tinkle"; a drink was a "sharpener" and when he offered me a second, I'd hear him say "a bird cannot fly on one wing." Whisky was "nig". Referring to an old man, he would say "He's got one foot in the grave and the other on a banana skin." And when you passed on, "you fell off the perch."

Upon John's death, one obituary read:

"A man is known by the company he keeps. The congregation

at St. Marks bore witness to him. It is certain every man and woman present in that great and distinguished congregation on that summer's morning was linked with some memory of good fellowship shared in his company. There were those whom he himself would have chosen to be with him in times both gay and grave. Life brought a full share of each."

A grave, wise thoughtfulness and truth,
A merry fun outlasting youth.

I can see Bill Jackman of Abingdon practically knee-deep in Maharaja's. They came from Kashmir, Baroda, Hydrabad and Patiale to buy their polo ponies from Bill, because they believed he was the best. And they were right to think so. He and his three daughters schooled the ponies to perfection and themselves made up a team.

I can see Bill Holman, that staunch ally of mine in the Middle East, remaining wonderfully calm in the midst of total confusion. When things went wrong, our Arab drivers did tend to wave their arms around a little. But the calmness of Bill would be contagious. In no time at all, the babel of sound would fade away and peace return. By and large, horses like the quiet men.

And certainly no one understood horses better than Bill Holman. His grandfather trained no less than three Grand National winners, Freetrader (1856), Little Charley (1858) and Avatis (1860), plus four Cheltenham Grand Annuals in 1841, '42, '43 and '47. Bill's grandson, David Nicholson (top jockey and trainer) carries on the tradition.

I can hear again the laughter of Spencer Fishe, my Newmarket companion for 40 years. Spencer was one of those fellows who've done a bit of just about everything. He had ridden round-ups in Nebraska and Arizona; hunted possom with coon dogs in the Deep South; and been a show-jumping star in Madison Square Gardens. He had also worked in Hollywood during the days of the silent screen, driving the team in Ben Hur. To do this, he had lain flat, hidden beneath Ramon Navarro who held the dummy reins. A most hazardous exercise, but Spencer didn't seem to think so. "The directors were a bit difficult to work with," he said. "But the horses were all right. I understand horses."

I remember too the oceanic contentment of Harry Asselburgh, as he taught dressage at Porlock in Tony Colling's day. Here was a man being paid for the pursuit of pleasure. Sheer bliss! He is perhaps best known for his clever training of a tandem ride he produced at Olympia about 1939 and trained at Lady Yule's residence. The horses were ordinary hunters and had never previously been in a closed school. The riders were unskilled too. He also produced a Quadrille in seventeenth century costume. Dame Mary Colvin has kindly reminded me of these details, having herself taken part.

Another Newmarket man whose company I much enjoyed was Bruce Hobbs. After eight years with Cecil Boyd Rochford, Bruce fell temporarily out of love with racing in the early sixties. He then joined my firm and we were naturally delighted to have him with us. But I did feel that it was a terrible waste of talent. So when an offer came from him to go to Bedford House, we waved him farewell with regret, but understanding. Our loss was most definitely racing's gain.

And last but not least, I treasure the memories of my friend, Jabey (Jack) Barker who lived at Stevenage for many years. He had some good horses in his time, including Prince Hansel, Prince Basle, War Hero and All Red. But it's not for these that I remember him. He was the most generous man in thought and deed that I ever knew. And in his case at least, the fates were just and kind. He had set out in life with a pony and cart collecting scrap iron. And at the close of a particularly bad day at Hendon, he shouted to the pony to choose its own way. After a couple of lefthand turns, it took him into an aeroplane factory compound, halting in front of an enormous heap of scrap aluminium. That proved to be the turning point in his life, the beginning of a road that led to a fortune. And it really couldn't have happened to a better man. Jack died at Frinton-on-Sea where I now live.

Most of these old friends have moved on to a better world. And when my time comes, I like to think that they will all be there to greet me.

CHAPTER EIGHTEEN

RIDE ON BY

Footfalls echo down the Avenue
Down the passage we did not take
Towards the door we did not open
Into a rose garden.

T. S. ELIOT

I see the jockeys go by in their shiny new limousines. They look younger and more sophisticated than the big-time riders I first knew. The Rolls and the Bentley, chariots of the early champions, have been replaced by sleeker and sportier models. And they, of course, earn the kind of fortunes which the Danny Mahers and the Steve Donoghues would have regarded as the impossible dream.

And yet in a way nothing has changed. I can listen to the jockeys and it's as though half a century has faded away. Their world is still centered around that most constant of creatures, the horse. And because the horse hasn't changed, they haven't either. Their life still consists of early morning gallops, a long afternoon of racing, the drive home and early to bed in preparation for an almost identical day. There is little time for socialising or studying the big, wide world outside. They are part of the kingdom of the horse and most of them are glad to be so.

For some time I've felt a certain kinship and to no one more so than Tommy Weston, if only because I sorrow for him. He was potentially such a big talent and his retirement has not been perhaps very happy. He lived so much of his life under the shadow of his friend Steve Donoghue and whenever he talks of Steve, you'll still hear the awe in his voice.

I once asked Tommy whether he'd every realised that, at his best, he was as good as any man alive. He gave the question a little thought and then he said, "There were days when I went down to the start knowing that the race was mine long before the tapes went up and on such days I felt invincible."

Then he paused and added, "But they didn't come to me very often. I was always a bit short on belief."

His winning ride on Hyperion in the Derby of 1933 was regarded by many as one of the most polished performances ever seen at Epsom. Yet Tommy will have none of that.

"Hyperion was the greatest of them all," he says, daring me to say otherwise. "I just went along for the ride. It didn't matter who was on his back. He would still have won."

That wasn't the way Steve Donoghue saw it and that wasn't the way I saw it either. Together Tommy and Hyperion were a wonderful combination, but they needed one another. And the truly sad thing is that the rider never gained the fame and fortune his talents deserved.

Two miles up the road from my home lives another jockey for whom I've always had the warmest regard . . . Harry Carr, for so long the Queen's jockey. Harry was always a fine horseman, but the jewel in his crown was loyalty. His stable had lean patches as stables do. But the idea of switching to another would never have crossed this man's mind.

I am forever seeing such and such a jockey described as a horse lover. Unfortunately it isn't always true. A great many regard them as little more than machines. But Harry, at least, has always been very fond of them.

He lives with his wife Joan at the Genesis Green Stud Farm and although selling is his business, he has never enjoyed seeing them go. There was one to whom he was particularly attached and each year he would send it down to the Newmarket Sales with an impossible price upon its head. This puzzled me and so

I asked Joan why he did it. She smiled and shrugged, saying, "He feels he has to make the gesture. But he'll be terribly upset, if anyone ever buys it."

During the hey day of Persian War, the Champion Hurdler would spend his summer holidays at Genesis Green. And when his career was over, Harry offered to give him a home for the rest of his days. I only hope the old horse knows how lucky he is.

But when one talks of jockeys in Newmarket or, for that matter, anywhere in the world, the talk inevitably centres upon Lester Piggott. He stands out so high above the crowd. He's such an enigma that he intrigues us all.

I once saw him seated on an otherwise empty bench at London Airport in the early dawn of a Sunday morning. He wore cavalry twills and a black leather riding jacket. He had a grip bag at his feet, out of which poked the handle of a whip. And watching him sitting there, remote and solitary, I really felt that this must be the loneliest man in the world that day. He is recognised universally as the greatest jockey of his day. Some say of any day. Yet when he talks of happiness, I still wonder whether he even knows the meaning of the word. The smile of Piggott is a rare and fleeting thing. He will come riding into the unsaddling enclosure after his finest triumphs with that pale, stone face of his. The cheers of the crowd seemingly mean no more to him than the jeers he has suffered at odd times in the past. And all the while, he is on this apparently endless world tour, driven on by some ruthless, nameless ambition that feeds upon itself. For him, one season blends into another. For twenty-five years, he has been chasing the sun, heading for America, Australia, Jamaica, India or wherever, once the European season has run its course.

He does take the odd fortnight in Nassau with his family and has every intention of stretching out on the sands and watching the world go by. It rarely works out that way. In no time at all, he is making plans for the season to come, placing telephone calls around the world. At the first whisper of a good ride in Miami or Kingston, he will be off again.

At one time it was claimed by fellow jockeys that he did this simply because he didn't dare stop . . . that the first real rest he took would be his last. There is some truth in this. With a natural bodyweight of ten and a half stone coupled with the need to stay around eight-stone-six, he can't afford to let the poundage fluctuate. As it is, he lives on what many of us would regard as a starvation diet and smokes endless cigars to chase away the hunger pains.

But there is more to his endless chase than this. We all, to a certain extent, wrestle with our demons. Lester's demons just happen to be bigger, fiercer, more complex than most. To even begin to understand him, one must go back to school days. While still a tot, he went to a boarding school with considerable handicaps. He was partially deaf and he had an impediment in his speech.

He had great difficulty in understanding the other boys and they had even greater difficulty in understanding him. He even had this problem with the teachers themselves and consequently his marks were often low. He first raced when he was twelve and he picked a bad moment to arrive. For this was the end of a great riding era and all the top jockeys were growing old together. The last thing they wanted was a precocious boy — and Lester was certainly that — to remind them of the fact.

It was a stage in his life when desire far outran ability. The talent was there, clear for all to see, but he was in too much of a hurry. The senior jockeys tried advice, warnings and threats in that order. All were equally unsuccessful. At times, it got a bit rough out there with Lester handing out as much as he got.

"All he needs to do is see daylight, and he'll try to go through," one disgruntled jockey told me.

There were various talks with the Stewards and in the end, they stood him down. But by then the character of the man we know today had been forged.

Circumstances turned him into a loner at school and circumstances again had given him a lonesome role on the racecourse. It had hardened him too. Only the rash and the foolish deliberately crossed swords with him. As the new rising star, he could very easily have become popular, but this was an art he never bothered to acquire. It would appear he is totally indifferent to the opinions of others. Nor does he allow sentiment to cloud his judgment.

One year, there were two outstanding horses in the Two Thousand Guineas, Sir Ivor and Petingo. Sir Ivor was trained by Vincent O'Brien . . . Petingo by Sam Armstrong, Lester's father-in-law. As a freelance, he had the choice of both. He rode them both in training, pondered briefly and then elected to climb aboard Sir Ivor. He had judged him fractionally the better horse. It was as simple as that.

On raceday, Sir Ivor confirmed that judgment and this is an important part of the Piggott legend. He is rarely, if ever, wrong when it matters. There is just one place where the image of the cold, calculating, unsentimental man gets dented a little, and that's at home. His two daughters, Tracy and Maureen, treat him on terms of complete and affectionate equality. If he sinks into an armchair at the end of a long, hard day, they will scramble all over him. And he will suffer them gladly . . . for them, the most tolerant of men.

This side of the man is so surprising, so out of character with everything else you know about him, that you begin to wonder about the rest. On one count, there can be no doubts . . . his stature as a jockey. He breaks all the established canons. With the longest legs and the shortest stirrups in the business, he shouldn't by rights be able to stay on a horse. At times, he comes close to standing on its back, circus fashion, and only the most incredible balance keeps him there.

He is a man with no fresh worlds to conquer; on the mountain peak with nowhere to go, but down. He says that he will continue riding, until the pleasure goes away. And unbidden comes the thought . . . is this the one thing he's really scared of. Without racing, just how would he fill his days? Ever since his ginger-beer days, racing has been his life. He has known no other.

I believe my old friend Danny Maher would have understood that fear all too well. These two great horsemen, the greatest I've known, have helped to bring my life full circle. To compare their lifestyles would be to compare the night to the day.

But they had one common, all-consuming bond. To them both, a world without horses would seem a very empty place indeed. It would to me too.

The evenings are the best time of the day for old men such as I. Come the twilight, come the dreams. I have only to see the horses and riders going by . . .

APPENDIX

SADDLERY

This appendix is mainly to do with saddlery and the items mentioned are mainly connected with those my old firm had either popularised or had some special connection with. The firm began as Distas Limited and later, after the Second World War, became F. E. Gibson (Saddlers) Limited. The latter is still going strong at Newmarket, though I have now no connection with it at all.

The book *Saddlery*, by E. Hartley Edwards, has embraced many more items and could be called a text book on saddlery. This book can be recommended and is available in most libraries. The author acknowledged in his book that he gained a certain amount of basic saddlery data, and perhaps horse knowledge, from me, so I do not attempt here to duplicate what is already in Edwards' quite exceptionally good book.

WALSALL

Walsall is the home and centre for saddlery accessories as well as making a large number of saddles. Although we saddlers always prided ourselves on taking a little longer over making our own saddles than did the Walsall manufacturers, it is true to say that if you paid a good price for a Walsall saddle you could expect good quality. They, however, preferred an order for at least half a dozen saddles of one identical shape and size and we often had to make "specials" ourselves — having obtained the tree, on which saddles are made, from the maker. Hardware such as bits, buckles, stirrup irons and the "trees" were all made in Walsall in my time and leather was also dressed there.

The old-fashioned way of making a tree was somewhat

primitive — because the craftsman hacked the tree out of a lump of beech with a draw-knife. The beech having the peculiar grain which makes this possible. Just before the Second World War a man called Wright started to experiment and made a few trees with a three ply wood. This particular method failed.

The tree makers of the old beech type used to go to Gloucestershire and purchase coppice grown beech — planted very close together so there were few branches. By this means the grain was uninterrupted and therefore easier to shape.

The tree makers in Walsall had a wide range of customers in the old days. For years they sent trees to Australia, New Zealand, America, South Africa, Rhodesia, Italy, China and even Russia and Iceland.

The stirrup leather bars on good trees were made from 40-ton high tensile steel and so were unbreakable but the little spring loaded end was an expense really not required though always fitted — except when a hook bar was used — for no horseman with a grain of sense ever rode with them up in case he had a fall and the leather was not free to slide off.

After the Second World War an entirely new tree was brought out by some friends of mine — which altered the whole aspect of tree making. This was a laminated tree and is in use today. It has the advantage of being so constructed that it is resilient in itself and will receive tacks for the webs. I remember Billy Beebee, a retired tree maker — who is a friend and helped me with the Toptani tree — telling me whilst I was on holiday with him how he became frustrated with the amount of good beech wood lying about which was waste from the old type trees. So, being of an ingenious nature, he made his firm a machine to make wooden door handles. These sold well till, I suppose, plastic handles became more common and wooden ones were no longer popular.

FORGING

The reason there were so few hand forgers dates back to the

last century when there was a prolonged strike of these skilled men. Many of them worked in their own little back yard buildings, standing at the fire and vice for years on end, probably with only an odd day's holiday (to Blackpool illuminations) a year, and were grossly underpaid. They left their trade and took up other work and the big firms started casting bits, stirrup irons and the like in better metal than had been the practice. Necessity being the mother of invention.

Thus Adonis-Kangaroo and Eglentine metals became popular and seldom broke and then later cast stainless steel was used as it is today. No manufacturer of cast metal would dare arrange for his name, or the name of the metal, to appear on the item unless he was pretty sure of the quality of the casting.

The best metal obtainable for bits of stirrup irons is hand forged stainless steel. Hand forged steel is good but requires burnishing and these metals are hard to obtain.

So, we rely on cast stainless steel which is popular and in general use today and one hears of very few complaints. In addition, aluminium stirrup irons are very essential in racing where weight plays a prominent part.

BLINKERS

Many purchasers of blinkers do not appreciate that the eye-cups vary. A knowledgeable trainer will tell you when ordering them whether he wants a full cup, known as a three-quarter, or a half-cup, or a wide-awake. The latter gives almost, but not quite, full vision, only preventing the horse from not seeing another animal coming up alongside. These and the half-cups are particularly popular for hurdlers and steeplechasers.

Television commentators, excellent as they are and much enjoyed by people like me, sometimes get a little mixed up with the different head coverings and call blinkers "hoods". But a hood is a complete head and neck covering and is used to keep a horse warm. A nightcap is a shorter version of a hood and worn by racehorses at exercise during the colder months of the year.

Ted Molyneaux tells a story of riding a horse who usually jumped perfectly well but, when running and being pretty sure of winning the race, suddenly failed to negotiate the last two hurdles and was beaten. On examining the blinkers after the race, the eye-cups were found to be blocked with mud thrown up by a horse or horses in front at the time.

Recently blinkers have been made and used in America, which have an aperture at the rear of the cup and it would seem this is intended to allow dirt, dust or mud to get blown through to clear the cup and give vision.

Sometimes a nightcap is made with ear-caps so that the violent noises heard on racecourses can be diminished. The ears can also have cotton wool placed in them to add to the exclusion of noise.

Some years ago, a racing correspondent wrongly described blinkers as "the Rogue's Mask", which description was well discounted by Tim Fitzgeorge-Parker in his book *Training the Racehorse*. Tim starts his book on the subject of blinkers and goes on to describe the great use Atty Persse, the very successful trainer, made of blinkers when he was Tim's assistant trainer. Atty used them on nearly all his older horses and brought off some memorable coups.

Just as "winkers" were considered essential on carriage horses, so blinkers are a good means of keeping a horse's mind on the operation in hand. They are also used for horses liable to rear.

A pair of special eye-cups were made for Bruce Hobbs. He had a horse which objected to going under the old-fashioned starting barrier. By fixing eye-cups the horse was prevented from seeing above him and was, therefore, cured of this annoying trait.

My own firm were, I think, the first saddlers to fit elastic "inserts" to the straps which hold the blinkers in position. Later, we fixed quick release hooks which make the trainer's job in fitting blinkers on at the last moment in the paddock, perhaps on a fidgety animal, less of a trial.

Atty Persse reckoned that blinkers could improve a horse by as much as two stone and cited the case of his dual Jubilee winner, Durante. The latter was quite useless without blinkers, but was as genuine as they come, like Felicitation, Alycidon, National Spirit and many others, who have been similarly equipped.

Basically, Atty would say, they help to provide the impulsion once produced by the legs, but lost when jockeys started to ride with short stirrup leathers.

In America, where the tracks are all virtually identical and horses are not only raced, but trained on them, the animals not unnaturally get bored so that the vast majority of American horses have to run in blinkers.

Reverting to the full-length hood, this is a survival of the days when thoroughbreds were so robust, that they had to be sweated in their work, totally covered in clothing with hood, breast-piece and long heavy sheet.

Blinkers can provide too much impulsion and make a horse too "free". But in general their use is beneficial, saving the wearer a number of unnecessary hidings. The late Eph Smith was riding Royal Charger as a two-year-old for the equally late Sir Jack Jarvis. The colt was equipped with blinkers for the first time, but Jack ordered his jockey on no account to hit him. In the event Eph was beaten a head when the slightest tap might have won the race.

Jack was livid. "I know I told you not to hit him," he shouted at dear little Eph. "You could at least have waved it at him."

Eph shouted back: "What the bloody hell's the good of waving it at a horse in blinkers? He can't bloody see it!"

But one thing is certain. Blinkers can have such an effect on a horse, that one reform is long overdue in this country. Like the Turf Authorities of the other major racing countries, the Jockey Club should rule that, once a horse has won in blinkers, he should never again race without them.

SHOW SADDLES

The English Show saddle is, in my opinion, open to a certain amount of criticism. Having had experience in their use and success and the making of same, I feel I can at least say what I think.

Many times hunter judges, like Neil Foster and earlier Tom Wickham-Boynton, have expressed their dissatisfaction with the saddle. And many have said — perhaps early in the day at some big show — how they would soon be expected to gallop round a slippery ring, surrounded by a large crowd of spectators, upon a straight-fronted flat-seated saddle with no place for their knees or "behinds". This saddle deceived nobody into thinking the horse had a bigger "front" than was really the case.

How very much better would it be to use a saddle, as Drage's — the hunter dealers — always did, upon which a judge could have a really safe and comfortable ride, instead of a very straight fronted one, some even cut backwards, to give even less room for the judge's knees. From a letter recently received from Colonel Foster I gather there are less straight fronted saddles in the show ring today.

Tom Wickham-Boynton, father of Marcus Wickham-Boynton now a well known breeder of race horses, would frankly express his dislike of such a saddle before mounting, and dear old Frank Wilkinson would go so far as to ask for an ordinary hunting saddle to be supplied so he could comfortably evaluate the horse's capabilities.

Now I have on many occasions made a very good show saddle, or what we saddlers called a "dealing man's" saddle. This sat firmly on the animal's back as far back as the anatomy permitted, with extended bars, a girth strap on the point of the tree to fix this behind the all-important muscle and, with the sternum curve — hopefully well back (as in a really well made horse and is where the girth comes), the horse appeared to have more in front than he really had.

As regards the flaps these would not be dead straight but

would have a happy curve (not sufficient to lose a horse any prize) and a very neat roll to accommodate beneath the riders knee. The tree would be specially made with a slight dip and certainly not a flat seat, to take the seat of the rider.

Robert Orssich, to whom one would not tend to give advice for he was wise in such matters, always, to the best of my recollection, used a converted Owen Saddle. This he used with success on show hacks and hunters.

Although I personally prefer a straight headed saddle — cut back saddles do fit some horses best and at one time, and always in America, a 4" cut back saddle was used by some people. These are called "Lane Fox" saddles, but by reason of the 4" cut back are thick on the "twist" — the part immediately in front of the crotch.

The Americans use these "Lane Fox" saddles with flaps cut backwards, and as the riders ride very long on their three-gated horses the flaps being straight it doesn't matter.

One must always remember that the sternum curve does play an important part as to whether a saddle is going to stay where you require it. So often one sees a rider as soon as he has been pulled into the centre of the ring, quickly undo the girth and push the saddle hopefully back and then tighten the girth again before the judge mounts. Harry Faudel-Phillips, a great showman, always used to get me to sew in a piece of hairy fabric into the panel of the saddle to help keep the saddle in the desired position. Girths also had pimple rubber sewn into the part which came in contact with the sternum curve.

If you wish to know some more about show saddles and the fitting of these ask Jack Gittins next time you see him! However, if you have a good horse with good shoulders do not worry too much about the show saddle — just use a saddle which will let the judge enjoy his ride if possible and remember — do not supply a pair of small slippery irons which need rejagging.

I always remember an incident concerning a judge who was a rider who pressed his foot down extremely firmly with the ball of his foot. The judge, having just mounted a hunter which was being shown that day, pressed down his foot as usual. The stirrup had a slippery tread and the result was that the iron flew forward and struck the horse on the jaw, which was not a good start for his ride!

To go back to Tom Wickham-Boynton. This Yorkshireman was a most beautiful horseman and good man to hounds, and it was always a pleasure to have him ride one's show horse as a judge, which he accomplished usually a good deal better than one could oneself.

Sometimes a dealing man, and we dealt with many of this fraternity, would say they had a favourite saddle which fitted every horse. I remember Arthur Brake, the West Country dealer, telling me this and getting me to copy it, and which we did to his satisfaction.

On another occasion a certain dealer gave me a saddle for repair, which he said was a universal good fitting saddle. No wonder. When we got this saddle back and opened it up, we found the head of the tree was cracked and giving and taking, hence the reason for its popularity.

It was a difficult job to know quite what to do because if I had pulled the head into its original shape it would not have fitted so many withers. So I called in the late Mr. Wootten, the Newmarket Shoeingsmith who did our metal repairs. He was most helpful and I got him to put in a mild steel place so the head did not collapse altogether, leaving it much as it was and hoped for the best.

AERBORN RUG

The Aerborn rug did start with my firm and we were the sole suppliers for some considerable time by arrangement with the manufacturers of the rug.

Everybody knows how popular they are today and many people, as I do, realise the warmth obtained by placing some garment on the top of this net material, thus sealing the heat in each hole of the net.

When we see on television, as we do almost daily, travelling head lads throwing an Aerborn rug on one of his horses after a race, it is really — so far as warmth is concerned — a bit of nonsense. Without a rug on the top it will produce no warmth and the most it can do is to act as a "sweat" rug. Yet it is popular.

There lies quite a story behind the Aerborn rug. The idea came from a far-sighted lady holidaying in Norway who saw fishermen's wives making vests for their menfolk who were making and repairing their fishing nets. At least, this is the story I have been led to believe and I'm sticking to it! On returning to England she approached a helpful firm of Midland manufacturers who were prepared to make the Aerborn rug.

My arrangements with the manufacturers were quite satisfactory and my firm popularised the rug and were, for some years, the sole suppliers and I think we did our job quite well. However, after sometime, the makers, perhaps rightly, thought the demand should have increased even more and thought that, as we were retailers perhaps we were, in a way, holding up a universal sale. I believe the manufacturers got various people to approach saddlers in different parts of the country to examine the situation. Bath, I do know, was visited, and Newcastle and some other town. A saddler in each case was asked to supply an Aerborn rug, but there was no eagerness to supply and one saddler even asked if the person making the enquiry really wanted to buy one of those Gibson gimmicks! So, we gave up being sole suppliers in return for certain advantageous discounts and now everybody finds this satisfactory.

What, however, is odd is that users of rugs do not use the Aerborn for its real function — and for which I myself use the netting material (i.e. a vest) — to keep warm and why, therefore, horse owners do not put one under a standing rug either in place of, or in addition to, a 7 or 8 lb. blanket I cannot make out.

This brings me to standing rugs.

STANDING RUGS

Standing, or night rugs, when I first entered business were mainly made of jute, either plain or twilled, and as there were at least eight different qualities available to the wholesale horse clothing manufacturers it was difficult to compete for sales. So, remembering that the very best and discriminating customers used a different material altogether — the material sailing ships used called Sail Cloth — and to save any further argument as to who was selling the best standing rugs I began to sell the Sail Cloth rug. I can claim, I think, that I was mainly responsible for popularising this type of rug.

Further, my firm added eyelet holes for fillet strings and a carefully padded surcingle and were very careful in the cut, leaving plenty of room at the withers, where much soreness arises. But more about withers elsewhere.

The Sail Cloth rug is very good value, hard wearing, wind and shower proof and stands up to washing and the dealing men liked it because when their names and addresses were stencilled upon the rugs, they stood out admirably.

Twilled jute was good also and very warm and the late Jock Crawford of the British Bloodstock Agency bought hundreds of rugs from us made to his own design with a breast strap in place of the usual front formation. The idea was that horses travelling in warm countries would be cooler. I can remember supplying this rug fully but loose lined in quantity for 12s. 9d. each — and each rug was stencilled with the initials of the firm on both sides and this, remember was good twilled jute material, next best to Sail Cloth.

In those days our rugs all had red unbreakable leather straps — this was a great advantage as this leather is practially impervious to water and so could be easily washed. Incidentally, the webbing of the surcingle, at any rate the front one, should be looped and padded over the spine so there is no pressure on the spine.

ROLLERS

The question of surcingles brings one automatically to rollers. This piece of equipment must be spoken of and how many of us have seen the tell-tale white patches on literally hundreds of horses? This is due to ill fitting rollers — either breaking or standing rollers — and it was, the late, polo playing Billy Balding of Rugby who really gave this matter deep consideration. He was the originator of the steel arch roller which bridged the spine completely. But here again the pressure, in my opinion, came too much on two particular places on the back and did not spread the load sufficiently.

The Balding family of Rugby for whom I had, and have, great respect made a great name for themselves in the polo world and now the name Balding is held in high esteem by the two young race horses trainers — Toby and Ian. Gerald senior, their father, was kind to me and, when he was playing polo so brilliantly in America, was quite helpful during the difficult times I experienced whilst employed in Pennsylvania.

However, Billy Balding never patented the roller or the girth though he discussed the matter of protecting his ideas with me at the Hunter and Pony Show at the Agricultural Hall, Islington, in the 1930s, but it was too late because once an article has been made and sold on the open market no Patent Agent can do anything for you. This was brought home to me with the red stirrup leathers, the Kimblewick Bit and several other "lines" my small firm produced and wished to protect.

As a firm we did in later years endeavour to improve the usual Arch roller by using a very light alloy and making the panel of the roller larger heart-shaped and hinged.

Hunting and Hack owners like rollers. They do improve the waistline and, of course, should be used with a breast girth for, by using these, the roller need not be tightened so much.

Many showmen in my time used cruppers attached to the rollers to keep the roller in the ideal position. This improves the waistline into which the saddle will, hopefully, sit. This is especially true when the all-important sternum curve, or hollow, is not pronounced — or what Jimmy Lindley, when commentating at Goodwood one afternoon in 1974, cleverly referred to as a "shallow rib cage" — and which does a great deal to keep a roller, and for that matter a saddle, in the correct place.

Some animals simply have no sternum curve and slope away. This was very obvious in a race I saw in 1974, when a filly probably lost because of her saddle slipping completely out of place — and losing a weight cloth into the bargain.

Perhaps I could respectfully suggest that the ordinary simple web breast girth is not the answer and that a light, full, breast-plate is much more likely to hold the saddle in place satisfactorily. I refer to a light and neatly made copy of the old hunting breast-plate, linked up to the girth between the fore legs.

So often in the past one saw in stables a roller on some horse placed upon a folded sack (sometimes two), just because the roller had lost all its shape and its two little panels allowed to become flat and which should have been stuffed up in an attempt to bridge the spine. The addition of sacks, or for that matter felt pads, do no good really and only sweat the back in a place where we want to keep the back hard, as the saddle will be placed there when the animal is ridden.

WALKER'S BENDING TACKLE

Major Johnnie Walker, the very well known veterinary surgeon of the 1920s and 1930s was at one time winning a great many prizes with show ponies. He was assisted in this by his daughter Norah (now Norah Bourne, the Judge). I noticed that the head carriage of their ponies was quite different to all other ponies being shown at that time.

Johnnie lived in Slough and I had an uncle living nearby who was acquainted with him. My uncle arranged a meeting and Johnnie then informed me how this head carriage was achieved. Johnnie had a set of almost amateur made bending tackle consisting of a bridle with special features including a four ringed half moon snaffle bit. The inside rings were connected to a nose and face piece which were connected to the side reins, which of course were adjustable. The outside rings were used only for driving. The roller (adjustable each side) was quite ordinary except that the side reins were not (except on certain occasions) attached to the roller as is customary with breaking tackle but went to an elastic quoit or brushing type ring on the rump on the crupper.

The dock was very large — lifting the tail and hollowing the back somewhat. The crupper was filled with linseed oil seeds, so when the crupper was used a certain amount of oil was secreted through the leather, thus making it comfortable for the pony's tail. To prevent the pony becoming over-bent, a most ingenious overcheck was used which consisted of a metal curb raiser in the curb groove, held in position by cord which ran from the curb raiser through the two inside rings of the four ringed snaffle, up the side of the ponies head to two pulleys and then to the rubber ring on the rump. This all sounds very complicated but believe me, if the owner had the patience and the aptitude to carry out the instructions, the ultimate result was well worth the trouble.

The fact that the side reins went clear of the roller meant that the whole of the pony's body was under tension and not merely the fore part, as is the case when the side reins go on to the roller. Of course it was a highly desirable piece of equipment for those who could be patient and able to "fiddle" with it.

An animal could have this tack put on and be left to walk about his box, flexing and keeping his head in the correct position and never sitting and sulking on the manger — so frequently seen when the usual tack is used. To start with only short periods were recommended.

I expect the Major knew full well no one could operate the set well enough to give him any opposition in the pony classes! It took a great deal of adjusting but those customers who really tried were very successful. The late Keith Lee-Smith, and others whom I have forgotten, where supremely successful in pony showing and were admirers of this equipment. Only recently, in 1975, Jennie Loriston-Clarke told me she still used a set. Her father and mother, the late Colonel and Mrs. Anne Bullen, bought a set from me and had instructed their children in its use. Jennie gave that superb performance in 1975 at Wembley riding Mrs. Steele's "Kadett" and is now, in 1978, in the forefront of our dressage riders.

Major Walker so very kindly allowed me to sell his bending tackle. It sold quite well and I well remember one year at Richmond Show selling seven sets in three days. I think this was mainly because I had a very beautiful skewbald toy model horse, covered with real pony skin and with the tackle on him, placed on a stand and this attracted a lot of people. It really was rather a lovely model which I had bought from Harrods. I understood from them that they had bought a few from Russia. My wife sold our one during the war.

The bending tackle could not really be called a financial winner, because one had to spend a considerable time explaining its features and trying to discover if the potential customer was not only competent enough, but also had the patience, to operate the set.

Perhaps I should explain here that I travelled many miles to demonstrate the set; only to find often that the person who had, should we say, given a firm order for a set at some show and who had been very excited about the purchase — which had not, of course, been paid for — had in the meantime been dissuaded from buying by some sceptical husband, or an old fashioned groom and so had lost interest.

I remember an occasion which was typical of many when a very rude gentleman (I hardly think that this is quite the right term) met me without even a "good morning".

"Oh, you are the man with the new breaking tackle!" And when I explained it was for use on broken, or very nearly broken, animals, he seemed not to understand and disappointed at least, for he had got a young unbroken colt waiting to test the set.

However, I did manage to give a successful demonstration

on a partly broken three-year-old and, to my astonishment, the "gentleman" accepted the set and eventually paid for it.

I admit that trade was difficult in the 1930s and that one was trying to sell to a public who perhaps in many cases honestly did not have any spare cash. However, we saddlers did stand to be shot at because so often people would spend half an hour ordering some special item of equipment — a saddle, bridle, roller, rug or whatever — and, of course, would not pay a bob. When they received the goods they had, what you could say, "gone cold" and sometimes without even hardly unwrapping the parcel, they would return it to me. Often merely by reversing the label and sometimes without a letter of explanation.

Frequently, I had to point out that it was quite impossible to reconcile their statement that a bridle "did not fit" when it was obvious the bridle had not at any time been put together.

The real value of Walker's bending tackle was in getting an animal to "flex" and obtain correct head carriage. I would say this without going into the matter too deeply and starting arguments with the High School ladies and gentlemen. There were many sets sold but a very small proportion were used correctly and the odd thing was that Major Johnnie Walker, Keith Lee-Smith and the Bullens who, to my way of thinking, were the great users of them, all had excellent child riders to ride for them and it was really to take the place of a child nagsman that we sold the sets.

It so happens that one successful racehorse trainer — the late Sam Hall — used this type of bending tackle at one time and also a coincidence that his father was a well known driving horse enthusiast. Driving men have seldom been much good to saddlers for such equipment because they are clever enough to "fiddle" their existing tack to obtain the result they need. You couldn't tell Cynthia Haydon or her husband much about rollers, overchecks and such devices!

The difference between our saddler's tackle and the harness man's contrivances was that we endeavoured to elevate the horse's head by the "curb raiser", and not by an overcheck bit in the corners of the animal's mouth.

In conclusion, I would say Walker's tackle was best understood by persons who had come to realise that the secret of any horse's good mouth is to transfer pressure from the nose to the bit gradually when breaking. With his tackle such a result could be achieved.

RED STIRRUP LEATHERS

I came across red buffalo hide stirrup leathers in Leeds around 1936. A friend of mine who used to make our Sail Cloth standing rugs and some paddock clothing, asked me to go with him to Hull Docks to see some leather being off loaded. We found it was buffalo hide leather and that it was being sent to some leather merchants at Keighley for use in the mills as a connecting link between the bobbins and the machinery. Anyway, I managed to get enough to make up three pairs or so of stirrup leathers and sent a pair to Bill Holman of Cheltenham, who was a customer and friend who happened to break stirrup leathers with great regularity.

This was an odd fact because the usual stirrup leather breaker was a short bulky man who rode too long and somehow snapped the leathers near the saddle bar, and yet Bill was tall and a good horseman.

Bill reported favourably and my firm started to sell these unbreakable leathers with great success though, of course, it was necessary to procure a really first-class buckle, otherwise we would be courting disaster on the assumption that a "chain is as strong as its weakest link".

I managed to find a maker of hardware in Walsall who would almost guarantee his buckles, and I remember the firm wrapped each pair up in tissue paper so highly did they regard them. I can say that with these particular buckles we never had a break and never a question of a broken leather. These were Eglentine buckles, and had the tongue "recessed".

I have no doubt there are stirrup leathers in use today over thirty years old which will still be satisfactory. In fact only recently I was talking to Phil Oliver (Alan's father) about another matter and he said he still used a pair of my old red leathers and a standing Martingale, both of which were supplied in the 1930s.

I had the red buffalo hide tested at a northern University and the breaking tension was enormous, something like 28,000 lb. tension to one inch. This was quite phenomenal and unnecessarily strong, so I knew my firm were on to a very good thing. So we were the sole suppliers for years — in fact until another firm brought out a leather which was tolerably strong, and they had it dressed red so as to be an obvious copy of our make.

CRADLES

Cradles perhaps are not a very interesting subject and many people never, throughout their lives, have occasion to use them. Cradles are used to prevent a horse recently "fired" or "blistered" from getting his mouth to his legs.

The usual cradle consists of about ten "turned" pieces of wood (ash) strung on straps and placed round the animal's neck collar-wise so he cannot bend his neck. These have been in use for time immemorial.

My firm produced one called a "Cheshire" cradle, which we thought was a great improvement. This was a bow made of metal which sat on the horse's front just above his brisket, with a piece of metal curved up to his headcollar where it formed a "U" shape and was strapped to the squares at each side of the headcollar.

The Cheshire was reasonably popular when displayed at shows and for years I thought it was the best possible cradle and most useful for a horse which chewed his rugs.

A third type — an American pattern similar to the Cheshire — was popular and one I had seen always in use when I was in America. It was made of aluminium and only weighed 3 lbs though it was not imported or copied so will be virtually unknown to English stables.

The simplest cradle was used by Bobby O'Neill the well known Cheshire veterinary surgeon, now partially retired. This consisted of a good-quality ash broom shaft which was attached to the headcollar and between the animal's legs to his roller. No doubt with some suitable straps at the ends of the broom shaft.

Bobby's father was a very well known Irish horse dealer who brought countless animals over to England. He was a regular seller at Leicester Repository and I have seen him at York, Cheltenham and occasionally at Tattersalls in Knightsbidge. He was a great character and most popular, and had close connections with horse dealers in England, and especially with Jack Snowden the Starbeck (near Harrogate) dealer.

THE U.V.G. RADIUM COMPRESS

The U.V.G. Radium Compress, a German product, was introduced to me in 1932 by a friend and customer called Bill Kent. He married Dinah Heasman who rode hacks so successfully, and is the mother of the well known lady rider Jane McHugh.

The Compress consisted of a piece of gauze, into which minute particles of Radium had been impregnated, and had a jacket covering one side and a woollen material the other and the whole well bound. It supplied a small continual heat and was just the right size for a fore leg, and there were other sizes for hocks and so on.

Anyway my firm took it on, and many people found it highly satisfactory, but we met with some scepticism especially amongst the vets.

As saddlers, of course, we could not give as much of our selling time to it as the suppliers would have liked. However, it sold in limited quantities at £3. 15. 0d. per pad and I can remember Matthew Peacock using a pair for some well known horse troubled with sore shins and, like many other users, being very satisfied. I remember putting a pad on my wife's back at one time, as she was suffering from strain, and there was no question of its value. Nevertheless, I must admit there was always a "niggle" at the back of one's mind as to its real connection with Radium. Yet, certain substances did show up on the gauze if one looked at it in a darkened place and, anyway, it was odd how in the end its claims were justified.

After the Second World War, during which, of course, there had been no importation, we started to get enquiries for the Compress. Also Victor Saloschin, a German dressage expert, was very enthusiastic, and he popularised it.

In 1975, out of interest, I had an old U.V.G. pad tested for radium content and was informed it still had some remaining in it.

LEAD REINS

Possibly the uninitiated would not know much or be very interested in the number of different lead reins there are.

Up to a few years ago if one was watching a racecourse paddock scene on television, looking at the horses going round one could pick out any horse trained by the late George Todd or the late Tom Masson and now his son Mick Masson. The reason was that both used an extra long paddock lead rein, which goes right over the horse's poll. If the horse was to "go up" when fitted with this pattern his lad could restrain him on the head and not on the mouth. So sensible and so simple, yet only these two master minds tumbled to the fact.

All paddock lead reins are of the quick release variety and vary in length and width of tubular linen and webbing. The quick release device is attached to the two rings of the bit so one is pulling on the bars of the mouth evenly.

SUPPORT BANDAGES

Elasticized support bandages, and those made with no width-way spread are of numerous makes. I have tested many, including some sent to a friend of mine, from the large number used in America.

Some of the most recent ones have had Velcro fittings on the tapes (the material which sticks to its counterpart and is reasonably secure) which is a long way from the times when travelling head lads sewed on the bandages. The great fear with these bandages, placed on a horse about to race, is that of putting them on too tightly. Races have been lost because this has been done.

Tail bandages are sometimes put on far too tightly and there have been cases of horses on a long journey having had their tail mutilated and the skin and hair sloughed off in parts.

Stable bandages are usually 5 inches wide by 2½ yards long and are used for wearing in the stable as their name implies. They are applied to keep a horse's legs warm and to fine the joints.

Johnnie Harper, that first-class stableman, always put them on somewhat loosely (so as to concentrate on the joints and not to fine the leg below the knee). He always used squares of gauze tissue, neatly sewn round so they did not fray, and they lasted for weeks or even longer. This gauze was known in the old days as Gamgee tissue, made by a well-known firm in Chesterfield called Robinsons and Sons. (They are equally well-known today as makers of cotton wool.) The gauze was the brainchild of one Dr. Sampson Gamgee, F.R.S.E., Consultant Surgeon to the Queens Hospital in Birmingham about 1878. He wisely patented his product in England and in America. Later, he agreed to assign the patent and rights to Robinsons for £400.

We have Dr. Gamgee to thank for popularising a surgical dressing into which an antiseptic could be easily impregnated. Later, of course, sterile dressings were made and sealed. (Whilst reading various records concerning Dr. Gamgee the author of one book stated he was one of the first [if not *the* first] surgeons in Birmingham to have regularly washed his hands before operating or dressing a wound!)

It so happens that comparatively recently Smith and

Nephew, the makers of such well-known dressings as Elastoplast, have brought out a highly successful sealed, sterile, non-adherent dressing called Melolin which by reason of its make-up (having a perforated plastic layer) is useful for open wounds and goes a long way to prevent pulling off scabs when dressings are removed. The latter being something which as a rule has to be soaked off. The horse world I gather has yet to avail itself of this product.

TONGUE STRAPS

Customers frequently would come to me with their particular troubles regarding some horse they owned and the most common was undoubtedly a cure being required for "tongue over the bit", due usually to imperfect early training. Some animals have a tongue which is large and does not fit into the lower jaw. These animals are the most difficult to cure.

There are tongue straps to hold the tongue in place and one device I found very successful if correctly adjusted, consisted of a strap which went over the nose and was suspended from the noseband in the centre and each end had cheek guards which held the bit up in the horse's mouth, i.e. to the roof of the mouth. It was used with an unbroken snaffle.

This device tended to bring pressure on the nose, similarly to the Kineton, and which could be a good thing. I cannot remember many cases of failure with this contraption, always provided care was taken to fit it correctly.

A lighter and more delicate device was made for racing. Many people, of course, used grids and ports, put on an existing bit, but these sometimes prevented a horse putting his tongue over the bit. They did not give him more room for his tongue and he usually evaded it somehow.

Another habit, similar to tongue over the bit, is lolling and this and tongue swallowing has been the subject of much research by the veterinary profession. Sometimes an operation is performed, but I do not know how successful this has turned out to be. Many races have been lost through a horse acquiring, for some reason or other which I have never heard thoroughly explained, these unfortunate habits. The rubber, Australian type, "Cheeker", so widely used in racing today lifts the bit and brings pressure on the nose, but lolling, to my mind and to people with whom I have recently discussed the problem, feel it perhaps best left alone.

BITTING

In 1832 a Spaniard called Don Juan Secundo came to England with confirmed ideas about bitting. Based in London, he became to be known either by advertising or somehow else, as a great help to people experiencing difficulties with unmanageable horses. My information regarding his methods are limited, but it would appear that Secundo was most useful in the correction of tongue over bit troubles with curb bits and his idea of a mouthpiece was, in my opinion, very sensible because instead of putting some contraption on top of the mouth he made the mouthpiece so the tongue fitted into the port.

Secundo would arrive at some gentleman's stable and see the problem horse ridden and, perhaps, would ride it himself. Then, carefully measuring the animal's mouth and judging the length of cheek (which in those days was called a "branch") he would select the two parts of the mouthpiece and fit them together as the ends of the mouths were made with screw ends and quarter size nuts.

Later, bit makers dispensed with the inter-changeable method and made bits up in different sizes. These bits were often seen at sales in recent years and my old firm sold them on occasions. The late Dick Pritchard when living at Peterstow Court, Ross, and who was a dressage enthusiast, bought several from us and found them very satisfactory. It was fascinating to fit one of these bits to a horse's mouth and almost instantly see the tongue being accommodated in the "port".

CURSETZEE FLAT BIT

Major General Cursetzee a Parsee who was in the Indian Medical Service, hunted from Oakham for some years and was a customer of mine. One day he asked me if I would make up, and patent, a bit he had tried out in India.

The bit was extremely simple and was very useful at one time. It was an unbroken snaffle, but instead of being round it was flat and only 1/8" thick and 1¼" wide. In other words it was a flat piece of metal lying on the tongue and bars of the mouth and as any bit enthusiast knows, you govern a horse by placing pressure upon the sensory nerves and the wider the bit, the greater control is achieved. Being a flat bit, one can close a horse's mouth whereas with a thick bit, you cannot so easily do so. The Cursetzee bit gave a maximum amount of pressure and it had two slots at the top of the snaffle ring to prevent it from getting into the unlikely position of being edgeways on the tongue or bars of the mouth. I had it patented and paid the General a small royalty for every bit sold, but it had a limited sale.

THE PELHAM

About the same time that Cursetzee's flat bit was being sold the Americans produced a Pelham with a very similar mouth. This was called an S.M. and was popular with polo men. Many people thought this was the brainchild of the late Sam Marsh, a distinguished and versatile horseman, but this was a fallacy.

The S.M. had a mouth which could only revolve in the cheeks for a quarter of the full circle and therefore always lay flat upon the bars of the mouth and tongue.

Sam Marsh did produce a curious bit which he called Scamperdale, after his place of business, but this had a mouth like a door handle and the cheeks came down 2" behind the usual place, and so the horse could not attempt to hold the cheeks with his lips.

KINETON NOSEBAND

The late Pelham C. Puckle of Kineton was a very accomplished horseman. I first got to know him well when he brought out the "Kineton" noseband, known to most horsemen and, in my humble opinion, not really fully appreciated over the years. People who have failed to find it effective usually have themselves to blame because sufficient care has not been taken in its fitting.

The idea behind the Kineton is to bring restraint upon the horse's nose before, or at the same time — according to the severity of nose pressure required — as the bit. It is really a very ingenious device. Control can be increased, in my opinion, if a half moon snaffle bit is used in place of a broken one.

Puckle never succeeded in getting this device patented because, I imagine, he fell into the same trap as I did later with several items which could have been money spinners, by selling the noseband before applying for a patent.

I made him a number of little gags which he used to elevate a horse's head, and which worked very quickly and easily because I suggested he used greased cord in place of rolled leather, which has a habit of sticking.

The use of a nose net, so widely used in harness horse days, is sometimes used for a horse which is difficult to control. If you have read the earlier part of this book you will remember how a Hansom cabbie successfully controlled a difficult horse and won a fiver from my uncle during my young days in London. And how a trainer got his hard pulling horse to the start by use of a nose net.

Quite recently a young amateur rider wrote to me regarding a horse he could not prevent from dashing off in front of the field during a race. I suggested a nose net and it so happened I was watching television when the next race he rode in was being screened. He had fixed his horse with the nose net, and to my amazement, and feeling of guilt, the horse remained completely motionless at the start. The starter's assistant and his whip were unfortunately absent and so the horse failed to start. You could say the net "outfaced" him! Still, by trying out this device with care I believe the nose net can nevertheless be a great help.

WHIPS AND RIDING CANES

There are many "whips" in existence. For example, there is a jockey's whip, a driving and lungeing whip and a hunting whip — the word "crop" is not correct. And one could write at great length about the simple cane, usually carried by anyone closely connected with horses.

The cane most popular in my day, and maybe today, was the Nilgeri with root handle, sometimes part or wholly covered with pigskin. These balanced nicely and were "whippy" and long lasting.

The Whanghee cane, with root notches (actually it is the root of a cane and the notches are suckers beneath the ground), it is used today for ladies handbag handles, knife and fork handles. It is quite useless for hitting a horse, but does not slip through the fingers and, if you want something just to carry, are good enough.

Children's canes come usually from Ratan Cane. These are a pleasant colour and come in various strengths to suit individual people and purposes.

Malacca cane is used extensively for walking sticks with bone handles or silver knobs, dog whips and the stouter ones for drain rods.

Ash was used for inexpensive hunting whips and of course walking sticks, which you can often see for sale in tobacconists shops today.

Perhaps the most interesting cane is the twisted Micocoulier (sometimes miscalled vine) cane, used by schooling jockeys. The tree from which it comes is of the Nettle family. Information regarding all these canes and the trees from which they come I obtained from helpful people at Kew.

I have in my possession a very elderly whip made from the Lagetta tree which is found in Jamaica and Haiti. The Lagetta tree grows to some forty feet high and is remarkable for its inner bark, which consists of very many thin laminations which can be separated readily and present a striking similarity to fine lace. When made into a whip, this "lace" is sometimes left on a stock to act as a thong, as is the case with my own whip. It is said that the Governor of Jamaica presented Charles II with a cravat, frill and a pair of ruffles made from this bark.

HUNTING WHIPS

Most articles of sports equipment are, or should be, bought with great care and patience.

Hunting whips for years have been given as presents, both to adults and to young children on initiation into the pleasures of the chase. It is best for the person giving this present, if not wholly familiar with these whips, to go to a reputable saddler and obtain the expert advice of the salesman.

Most hunting men would insist upon choosing their own whip, thus ensuring that "balance" (they must "feel right"), length of stock and covering, probably plaited Kangaroo or plain pigskin, was to their liking. Then there is the hook — so important when you realise you may possibly have to catch a wet and heavy field gate to prevent it breaking your leg. The hook is made of buckhorn and the right curve is hard to obtain. Sometimes they are sold with a sharp pointed stud on the heel to help hold a gate, but I personally always found this type wore your breeches into holes.

The thong is usually 1¾ yards long and most hunting men prefer a fair amount of belly (thickness). The thong is plaited by using eight pieces of leather and to this is attached the lash of silk — or cord.

Now we come to the keeper, the part that links the thong to stock, and the average follower of hounds accepts the very neat type which consists of two pieces of leather, tapered and sewn. All very businesslike, but if you were a saddler selling a whip to a master hunting hounds, you would not make such a false move as to offer this type of keeper, because the loop type is essential for by-passing the thong through. Then you have a business-like collar for catching a hound or a fox for that matter, emerging from a drain or earth. I have frequently seen a horse who had become bridle-less being restrained by the same means.

Finally we come to the stock and what it is made from. This in the old days was good whale bone — and is nowadays good fibre glass — though the cheaper whips were made up from Malacca or ash, both quite satisfactory.

You will appreciate after reading the foregoing, that the purchase of a good hunting whip is not an item you would wisely obtain from some firm's catalogue unseen, but from a salesman who understands his job and with whom you can discuss your requirements.

A jockey's whip is, of necessity, a most important purchase for him, and when these little gentlemen have developed a certain style of riding they know what they want, weight, balance, leather handle or not and type of keeper.

The race whips were originally made of whale bone, and then in recent years the whipmakers turned their attention to fibre glass. After much experimenting there is now a good fibre glass whip on the market. The cheap whips are steel lined.

As regards lunge whips, I understand the most satisfactory ones in use are now made of fibre glass in Canada. These are made by a very ingenious method and usually have rubber hand parts. They are very strong and waterproof. They are known by their trade name — Wonder Whips.

I have always been keenly interested in walking sticks, so little used in these days. I have over the years collected some forty or more and one could write at length about them. These walking sticks are made from every conceivable type of wood, with a variety of handles and embellishments. There are horse measure sticks, sword-dagger sticks, and one stick I have contains two tubular glass flasks for spirit and water — for anyone requiring a "tot" on the way!

The tall thumb stick, used by the tweedy gentleman whilst

walking round his estate, came into popularity through the gamekeeper. He made them so a snake could be pinioned to the ground. Then the gamekeeper's master picked up one to walk home with and so they became popular and were to be seen in stick stands in the hall. My firm used to sell these and shepherds crooks, and the pleasantest thumb stick was always considered to be peeled chestnut.

For many years I purchased these from an amateur stick maker, and a very good one too, called Vincent Davies, who I remember first in Lancashire and later in Herefordshire. He is dead now, but I recall that buying sticks from this gentleman was a lengthy procedure as he would present them for inspection one by one and with each would give an explanation as to its type of wood. Each one was different and he certainly had got the art of producing a good stick. These were peeled chestnut, blackthorn, ash and hazel.

ACKNOWLEDGEMENTS

Many people helped me in the writing of this book and my thanks are due to all of them. In particular I would like to thank The Duke of Beaufort, Lorna Johnstone, Mary Phillips, Tim Fitzgeorge-Parker and Pepe Forbes.

I have mentioned in my text various books and articles and acknowledge the respective authors and publishers below:

The Riding Master, Jack Hance, (Robert Hale).

The Duchess of Duke Street, Daphne Fielding, (Eyre & Spottiswoode).

Horseman: The Memoirs of Howard Marshall, (Bodley Head).

Here Lies My Story, de Courcy Parry, (J. A. Allen).

Saddlery, E. Hartley Edwards, (Country Life).

Training the Racehorse, Tim Fitzgeorge-Parker, (Pelham Books).

The Times

The Field

Horse and Hound

INDEX

All references relating to saddlery are set in *italics*.
All horses' names are followed by (H).

Aerborn rug 101, 102
Alderson Sisters 40
Aldridges Horse Repository 29
All Purpose (dipped) Saddle 48, 74
All Red (H) 86
Altemus, Elizabeth 47
Armstrong, Robert 26
Armstrong, Sam 92
Armstrong-Jones, Anthony 81, 82
Asquith, Howard 50
Asselburgh, Harry 86
Avatis (H) 85

Badminton Horse Trials 83
Balding, Billy 104
Barker, Jabez 86, 87
Barnet, Tommy 42
Battleship (H) 47
Bayardo (H) 12
Beaufort, Duke of 82
Beebee, Billy 95
Beeby, Harry 30, 45, 47
Beery Method 29
Bertram Mills Circus 71
Bishop, Giles 33
Bitless bridle 50
Bitting 115
Blinkers 96-98
Bosca saddle 49
Bostwick, "Boy" 45

Bourne, Norah 105
Brake, Arthur 101
Briscoe, Basil 58-62
British Bloodstock Agency 103
Brown Tommy (H) 18
Bullen, Anne 107, 108
Bullen, Colonel J. 107, 108
Burghley Horse Trials 83

Canes, riding 118
Carr, Harry 9, 82, 89, 90
Carstairs, Carroll 17
Castlerosse, Lord 24
Cavan, Lord 21, 23, 24
Cavendish Hotel 16-19
Cazelet, Peter 51, 52
Champagne (H) 71
"Chanteur" 31
Cheeker 115
Cheltenham Champion Hurdle Race 61
Cheltenham Gold Cup 61
Cheltenham Grand Annual Race 85
Clarke, Ambrose 47
Colvin, Mary Dame 86
"Cosmaries" 72
Cradles 110, 111
Crawford, Jock 103
Crespigny, Claude Champion de, Sir 17, 18

Crown of Italy   22
Cundell, Frank   65
Cunningham, Alan, Major-General Sir   14
Cursetzee Flat Bit   116
Cuyer, Henri   71, 72

Davies, Vincent   121
Davy Jones (H)   51, 52
Dawson, Dick   41
Dee, Mary   72
Delmege, Hugh   64
Dixon, Oliver   30
Donoghue, Steve   9, 89
Durante (H)   98

Edward VII, King   9, 16
Edward, Prince of Wales   14, 21-23, 40, 61
Eglentine Buckles   109
Elizabeth II, Queen   82
Elliott, G. H.   30
Essex Hunt Cup, Colchester   18

Fane, Mountjoy   63, 66, 67
Faudel-Phillips, Harry   52, 53, 100
Felix II (H)   39
Fenn, Lilian   46
Field, Harold   35, 36
Fishe, Spencer   85
Fitzgeorge-Parker, Tim   97
Florizel II (H)   40
Forbes, Pepe   71
Forging   95, 96
Foster, Neil   99
Frazer, Doreen   11-13
Freeman, Will   9, 26
Freetrader (H)   85

Gamgee, Sampson, Doctor   113
Gamgee Tissue   113
Gibson, Alexander   29, 30
Gibson, Tuke and Gibson (bank)   25
Golden Miller (H)   51, 58, 60-62
Goldney, Major-General C le Bas   66

Grand National   51, 61, 85
Grantham, Tommy   9
Grieg, Louis   14
"Grunting"   30
Guards Divisional Artillery   14

Hall, Sam   108
Hance, Jack   48, 49
Hardy, Gaythorne   24
Harper, Johnnie   9, 26-28, 113
Haydon, Cynthia   108
Heasman, Dinah   53, 111
Hindley, Reg   49
Hitchcock, Tommy   18
Hobbs, Bruce   47, 86, 97
Hobbs, Reg   47
Hobday operation   65
Holloway, Sidney   44, 45, 47, 50
Holman, Bill   85, 109
Holmes, Harold   50
Hopkins, 'Boy'   49
Horse of the Year Show, Wembley   69, 70
Hyperion (H)   89

Insurance (H)   61
Irvine, Crystal   52, 53

Jackman, Bill   85
Jarvis, Jack, Sir   98
Johnstone, Lorna   71, 72
Johnstone, Rae 'Le Crocodile'   24, 82

Kadett (H)   107
Kent, Bill   111
Killarney (H)   72
Kineton Noseband   117
Kossmayer, Alphonse   71, 72
Kossmayer, Wenzel   72

Lancaster, Willie   30
"Lane Fox" Saddle   100
Leach, Noel   11, 13
Lee-Smith, Keith   106, 108
Lewis, Rosa "Duchess of Jermyn Street"   16-20

124

Lindley, Jimmy   104
Little Charley (H)   85
Llewellyn, Harry, Sir   76
Lloyd, Glyn   65
Loriston-Clarke, Jennie   107

McCalmont, Helen, Lady   50
McHugh, Jane   111
McIlwaine, Andrew   36
Maher, Danny   9-13, 15, 93
Margaret, Princess   81, 82
Marsh, Sam   116
Marshall, Mrs "Binty"   50
Martindale, Ted   34
Masson, Mick   112
Masson, Tom   112
Melolin   114
Metcalfe, "Fruity"   40
Middleton, Bay   18
Milburn, Devereux   18
Mildmay, Anthony   51, 52
Mills, Bertram   9, 47
Mitchell, Jim   24
Molyneaux, Ted   97
Morton, Mrs Dorothy   71
Moss, Johnnie   72

Needham, Robert   49
Nevett, Billy   42
Nicholson, David   85
Nightingale (H)   70
Noake, Joe   50
Nose net   30

O'Brien, Vincent   92
Oliver, "Phil"   110
Olympic Team, Helsinki, 1952   76
O'Neill, Bobby   111
Orssich, Robert   100
Osborne, Johnnie   26

Paget, Dorothy   58, 60-62
Paice, George   39-40
Parker, George & Son Ltd   74
Parker, "Goblin"   47
Parry, Bay   54-57
Parry, de Courcy ("Dalesman")   15

Payne, Bill   24
Peacock, Dobson   9, 41, 42
Peacock, Matthew   41-43, 111
Peatt, Ernest   65
Pelham ("S.M.")   116
Peralta, Angel   9, 69-71
Persian War (H)   90
Persse, Atty   97, 98
Petingo (H)   92
Phillips, Mary   71
Piggott, Lester   9, 10, 40, 90-93
Prince Basle (H)   86
Prince Hansel (H)   86
Pritchard, Dick   115
Puckle, Pelham C.   117

Radium Compress   111, 112
Red Stirrup Leathers   109, 110
Reins, Lead   112
"Rejoneo"   70
Reynolds, Charlie   9, 26, 32
Reynoldstown (H)   51, 52
Ribblesdale, Lord   19
Roberts, John   56
Robinson & Sons   113
Rollers   104
Royal Charger (H)   98
Rumsey, Charles   18

Sadler, George   35
Sail Cloth Rug   103
St. Leger Race   12
Saloschin, Victor   112
Saxby, Billy   24
"Scamperdale" Bit   116
Scott, Nat   26
Secundo, Don Juan   115
Show Saddles   99-101
Sir Ivor (H)   92
Sloan, Tod   12, 13
Smirke, Charlie   42
Smith, Eph   98
Smith, Harry "Swank"   42
Smith-Maxwell, John   84, 85
Smith & Nephew   113
Standing Rugs   103
Stanley, Lord   24

Steffany, porter at the Cavendish 18
Stella (H) 32
Stoddard, Len 18
Support Bandages 112-114
Sutton, Herbert 47
Sykes, Jack 72
Sykes, Joan 72
Sykes, Mary 72
Sykes, Nan 72

Tate, Ernest, Sir 42
Tattersalls 30, 49
Taylor, Joe 50
Temple Bar Riding Establishment 52
Thompson, Arthur 49
Tilke, John 72
Todd, George 112
Tongue Straps 114, 115
Toplis, Percy 55, 56
Toptani, Ilias, Count 9, 73-77
Townsend, "Mouse" 28, 58, 59, 65
Trees 94, 95
Trowers, Joe 34
Two Thousand Guineas Race 92

Walker, Johnnie, Major 105, 108
Walkers Bending Tackle 105-109
Walking Sticks 120, 121
Walton, Cliff 33, 34
War Hero (H) 86
Wardrop, General 21, 24
Watney, "Sandy" 64
Waudby, "Yorky" 42
Weaver, Leslie 64
Webb, Watson 18
Weetzen 76
Weston, Tommy 9, 88, 89
Whips, hunting 119-121
Whips, lunge 120
Whips, race 120
White, Wilf 76
Wickham-Boynton, Tom 99, 101
Wilkinson, Frank 27, 28, 99
William II, Kaiser 16, 17
Wilson, Gerry 61

Wood, Ann 37
Wootten, E 101

Young, Dick 24, 35

126